Traveling
California's
Gold Rush Country

by
Leslie A. Kelly

FALCON®
HELENA, MONTANA

A FALCON GUIDE®

Falcon® is continually expanding its list of recreational guidebooks. All books include detailed descriptions, accurate maps, and all the information necessary for enjoyable trips. You can order extra copies of this book and get information and prices for other Falcon® guidebooks by writing Falcon, P.O. Box 1718, Helena, MT 59624 or calling toll-free 1-800-582-2665. Also, please ask for a free copy of our current catalog. Our e-mail address is falconbk@ix.netcom.com and visit our website at www.falconguide.com.

All photos by Leslie A. Kelly unless otherwise noted.
Cover photo and color section by Leslie A. Kelly.

Library of Congress Cataloging-in-Publication Data
  Kelly, Leslie A.
      Traveling California's Gold Rush Country / by Leslie A. Kelly.
          p.   cm.
      Includes index.
      ISBN 1-56044-484-3
          1. California—Guidebooks. 2. Historic Sites—California—
      Guidebooks. 3. California—Gold discoveries. 4. Gold mines and
      mining—California—History. I. Title.
      F859.3.K45 1997
      917.9404'53—dc21
                                                              97-15108
                                                                    CIP

♻ Text pages printed on recycled paper.

CAUTION

Outdoor recreational activities are by their very nature potentially hazardous. All participants in such activities must assume the responsibility for their own actions and safety. The information contained in this guidebook cannot replace sound judgment and good decision-making skills, which help reduce risk exposure, nor does the scope of this book allow for disclosure of all the potential hazards and risks involved in such activities.

Learn as much as possible about the outdoor recreational activities you participate in, prepare for the unexpected, and be safe and cautious. The reward will be a safer and more enjoyable experience.

CONTENTS

Acknowledgments vi
Preface vii
Legend ix
Overview Map: California Gold Rush Country x
Chapter One—California's Gold Rush Country 1
    Discovery and Early History of California 7
    Post Gold Rush 8
Chapter Two—How To Use This Guide 9
    California Gold Discovery to Statehood Sesquicentennial 10
    Sleeping Where Presidents, Mark Twain, Bret Harte, and 49ers Slept 11
    The California Highway Patrol, 911, Stop Signs, Gasoline, and Deer 13
    Seasons and Topography 13
    A Few Caveats About This Guide and California's Gold Rush Country 14
    Private Property and Poison Oak 14
    Should You Decide To Become a Miner 15
    Mining Terms 15
    Errors and Omissions 18
Chapter Three—Organizing Your Tour of California's Gold Rush Country 19
    What To See in California's Gold Rush Country 19
    Touring California's Gold Rush Country in 1 Day on Highway 49 20
    Touring California's Gold Rush Country in 2 Days on Highway 49 20
    Touring the Northern Mines in 1 Day 22
    Touring the Northern Mines of Shasta and Trinity Counties 24
    Touring California's Gold Rush Country from San Francisco, Sacramento,
        Reno, Yosemite National Park, and Los Angeles. 26
    Touring All of California's Gold Rush Country 27
Chapter Four—Sutter's Mill: Where the Gold Rush Began 28
    Visiting Marshall Gold Discovery State Historic Park 31
Chapter Five—Mariposa County 33
    Mariposa 33
    Touring Mariposa 38
    Hornitos 38
    Bear Valley 40
    Coulterville 43
    Mariposa County Side Trips 46
    Yosemite National Park 46
    Ben Hur 46
    LaGrange (Stanislaus County) 46
    Mariposa County Travel Information 46

Chapter Six—Stanislaus County 47
    LaGrange 47
    Knight's Ferry 50
    Stanislaus County Travel Information 51
Chapter Seven—Tuolumne County 52
    Groveland 54
    Chinese Camp 55
    Jamestown 58
    Sonora 61
    Touring Sonora 64
    Columbia State Historic Park 65
    Touring Columbia State Historic Park 68
    Jackass Hill 72
    Tuolumne County Travel Information 73
Chapter Eight—Calaveras County 74
    Angels Camp 76
    Touring Angels Camp 76
    Murphys 78
    Touring Murphys 80
    Calaveras Big Trees State Park 83
    Sheep Ranch 84
    San Andreas 84
    Touring San Andreas 85
    Mountain Ranch 86
    California Caverns 87
    Mokelumne Hill 88
    Touring Mokelumne Hill 90
    Calaveras County Travel Information 91
Chapter Nine—Amador County 92
    Jackson 92
    Touring Jackson 95
    Chaw'Se Indian Grinding Rock State Historic Park 98
    Volcano 101
    Daffodil Hill 101
    Silver Lake 102
    Sutter Creek 103
    Walking Tour of Sutter Creek 104
    Amador City 106
    Drytown 106
    Plymouth 106
    Fiddletown 106
    Shenandoah Valley and the Amador Wine Country 109
    Amador County Travel Information 110
Chapter Ten—Mono County 111
    A Side Trip to Bodie State Historic Park 111
    Bridgeport 112
    Bodie State Historic State Park 112
    Mono County Travel Information 113
Chapter Eleven—El Dorado County 114
    Placerville 114
    Hangtown Fry 116
    Touring Placerville 118
    Georgetown 120
    Touring Georgetown 123
    El Dorado County Travel Information 124

Chapter Twelve—Placer County 125
   Auburn 128
   Side Trip to Foresthill, Deadwood, Michigan Bluff, and the Middle Fork
      of the American River 129
   Dutch Flat 134
   Placer County Travel Information 134
Chapter Thirteen—Nevada County 135
   Touring Grass Valley 136
   Touring Nevada City 140
   Touring Rough and Ready, Bridgeport, and French Corral 146
   Touring Malakoff Diggins 150
   Touring Washington and Truckee 151
   Nevada County Travel Information 151
Chapter Fourteen—Sierra County 152
   Touring Goodyear's Bar 153
   Touring Downieville 155
   Touring Sierra City 158
   Touring the Lakes Basin via Gold Lake Road 158
   Side Trip to Forest City and Alleghany 160
   Side Trip to Port Wine, Queen City, Gibsonville, Howland Flat, and Poker Flat 162
   Touring Loyalton and The Northern Terminus of Highway 49 163
   Sierra County Travel Information 164
Chapter Fifteen—Yuba County 166
   Touring CA 49 in Yuba County 166
   John A. Sutter and William Johnson 167
   Touring Marysville 169
   Side Trip to Smartville and Timbuctoo 170
   Side Trip on the Marysville–La Porte Road via Brown's Valley, Challenge,
      Woodleaf, and Strawberry 171
   Yuba and Sutter County Travel Information 173
Chapter Sixteen—Butte County 176
   Touring Oroville 178
   Touring Table Mountain and Cherokee 180
   Side Trip to Bidwell State Historic Park 183
   Butte County Travel Information 183
Chapter Seventeen—Plumas County 184
   Touring the Feather River National Scenic Byway 184
   Rich Bar 185
   Quincy 190
   Side Trip to Nelson's Point, Onion Valley, and La Porte 190
   Touring Plumas–Eureka State Park 193
   Beckwourth Pass, Beckwourth Trail, and Beckwourth's Cabin 194
   Plumas County Travel Information 196
Chapter Eighteen—Shasta County 197
   Shasta State Historic Park 197
   Shasta County Travel Information 198
Chapter Nineteen—Trinity County 199
   Touring Weaverville 199
   Touring the Trinity River Mining Camps 202
   Side Trip to Gold Bluffs Beach 202
   Trinity County Travel Information 203
Chapter Twenty—San Francisco: Town Built by Gold 204
   San Francisco Travel Information 205
Chapter Twenty-One—Sacramento: Dreams of New Helvetia and Sutter's Fort 206
   Sacramento Travel Information 207
About the Author 208

ACKNOWLEDGMENTS

Traveling California's Gold Rush Country is the product of more than 4 years of research and more than 40 trips of extensive travel in California's Gold Rush Country. I owe much to the historians, the staff of local and county travel bureaus and state parks, and to the local residents—some descendants of the 49ers who arrived in California during the Gold Rush—who provided me with assistance and suggestions for what should be included herein.

Extra assistance has been provided by a group of people who play a major role in the preservation and interpretation of historic sites and landmarks of California's Gold Rush Country. I have gained respect for what they do and owe deep gratitude for their patience while I have asked much of them during the preparation of *Traveling California's Gold Rush Country*. To these people I give a special "thanks for everything": Superintendent Matt Sugarman and Chief Ranger Rosanne Smith McHenry, Marshall Gold Discovery State Historic Park, Coloma; Jim Lenhoff of Oroville, Author and Historian; Kelli Coane and "Buzz" Baxter, Tuolumne County Visitors Bureau, Sonora; Tom Bender and Kathi Harvey of The City Hotel, Davy Stoller of Columbia Stages and Stables and Sherrin Grout, Ranger, Columbia State Historic Park, Columbia; Donald W. Haag, Mariposa County Chamber of Commerce, Mariposa; Ed Tyson, Searles Library, Nevada City; Catherine Kelly, my wife and travel companion on numerous trips to the historic inns and restaurants of California's Gold Rush Country and Erin Kelly, my daughter, for her proofreading of the manuscript.

Cover Picture: Visitors to Columbia State Historic Park can ride an old stagecoach, see an authentic Wells, Fargo, and Company Express building and shop in period stores just as the 49ers did. Columbia, Queen of the Southern Mines, is the only town in California's Gold Rush Country which has been restored to its Gold Rush-era appearance. Columbia State Historic Park is operated by the California State Parks System. Stagecoach courtesy Davy Stoller, Columbia Stage Line and Stable.

PREFACE

James W. Marshall's discovery of several small gold nuggets in the tail race of Sutter's Mill on the South Fork of the American River on January 24, 1848, changed the course of American, Mexican, and world history. Hundreds of thousands of gold seekers from all over the world joined in the rush to California to find gold in the creeks and rivers of the Sierra Nevada.

In two years, the former Mexican state of Alta California became the United States of America's 31st state on September 9, 1850. The Gold Rush forced the breach of the last great natural barrier to America's westward expansion, the Sierra Nevada. As gold fever swept the states and 49ers joined in the rush to seek the color, their sheer numbers, courage, and determination forged trails and roads over this once seemingly impenetrable mountain range.

Gold is still found in the creeks and rivers of California's Gold Rush Country, and the lure of finding nuggets still attracts hopeful miners to the Sierra Nevada. Most visitors come to relive those days vicariously by visiting the historic sites, seeking out accommodations in the remaining historic inns, and dining at some of the finest restaurants in California.

Historic buildings and sites remain for visitors to readily explore in Gold Rush towns such as Mariposa, Coulterville, Hornitos, Groveland, Chinese Camp, Jamestown, Sonora, Columbia, Angels Camp, Murphys, San Andreas, Mokelumne Hill, Jackson, Sutter Creek, Amador City, Drytown, Volcano, Placerville, Coloma, Auburn, Washington, Grass Valley, Nevada City, North San Juan, Downieville, Sierra City, Quincy, Marysville, Oroville, and Weaverville.

California will commemorate the sesquicentennial of the years 1848 through 1850 as the California Gold Discovery to Statehood Sesquicentennial with numerous special events in California's Gold Rush Country. For this reason, a visit during these 3 years will be especially rewarding because of the numerous commemorative events planned throughout California.

Traveling California's Gold Rush Country has been written and illustrated by Leslie A. Kelly to complement *California's Gold Rush Country* (Les Kelly Publications 1997, ISBN 0-9653443-0-4), the definitive coffee table book that presents all areas of California's Gold Rush Country with color photography of the spectacular scenic settings found there.

At the sesquicentennial of California's Gold Rush, *Traveling California's Gold Rush Country* provides information for visitors who seek to relive this era when the word "rush" was even more hectic than today's supposedly fast-paced lifestyle. Whether you travel in person or do so vicariously from your easychair, use this guide to follow in the footsteps of the 49ers through California's Gold Rush Country.

Replica of Sutter's Mill at Marshall Gold Discovery State Historic Park.

LEGEND

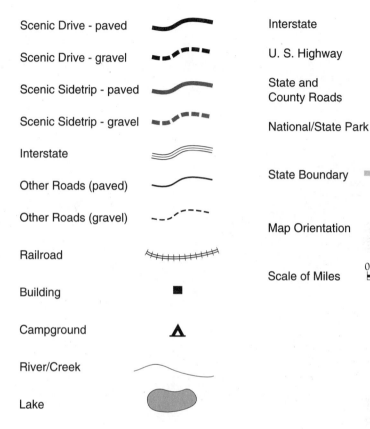

Scenic Drive - paved

Scenic Drive - gravel

Scenic Sidetrip - paved

Scenic Sidetrip - gravel

Interstate

Other Roads (paved)

Other Roads (gravel)

Railroad

Building

Campground

River/Creek

Lake

Interstate

U. S. Highway

State and County Roads

National/State Park

State Boundary

C A

Map Orientation

N

Scale of Miles

0   0.5   1

Miles

GOLD RUSH COUNTRY

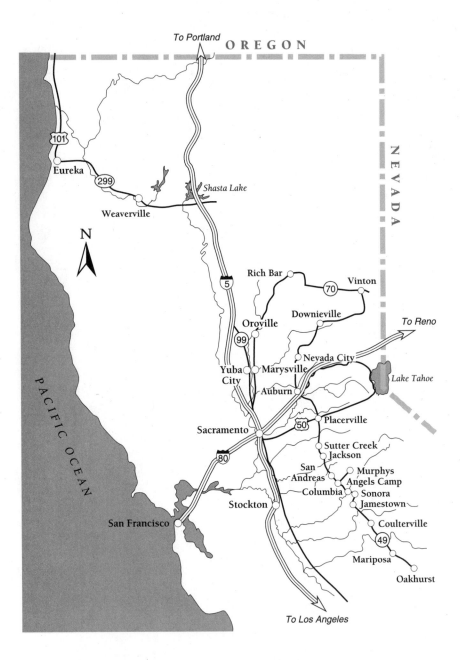

Chapter One

CALIFORNIA'S GOLD RUSH COUNTRY

Gold, gold, gold, from the American River!

"Monday 24th this day some kind of mettle was found in the tail race that looks like goald first discovered by James Martial the Boss of the Mill."

This simple entry, written by Henry Bigler in his diary on January 24, 1848, records the momentous discovery of gold at the edge of the South Fork of the American River by James W. Marshall. His was not the first discovery of gold in California. In the early 1840s gold was found just north of Los Angeles and in other areas of California. These finds were greeted with skepticism or received little attention. It was Marshall's discovery and the subsequent publicity by Sam Brannan that led to the California Gold Rush.

John Augustus Sutter, an emigrant from Switzerland, arrived in California in July 1839, with grandiose dreams and plans to establish a colony. In August, at the site of what would eventually become Sacramento, Sutter built a fort, which he named Sutter's Fort, and the settlement that developed in the area, New Helvetia. In 1841 he bought much of the equipment and livestock from the Russian Settlement of Fort Ross on the Pacific Ocean. To support elaborate plans for his colony, he expanded his activities to include Hock Farm on the banks of the Feather River near Yuba City and Sutter's Mill on the South Fork of the American River.

James W. Marshall was born in Lambertville, New Jersey, on October 8, 1810. Marshall gained experience as a carpenter and worked mostly in sawmills along the east coast before joining a wagon train for Oregon in 1844. In 1845, he arrived at Sutter's Fort and was immediately employed by John Sutter.

Marshall served with the Battalion of California Volunteers in the relief effort of Sonoma at the end of the Bear Flag Rebellio in 1846. He served until the end of the War with Mexico and distinguished himself at San Rafael and Los Angeles.

After the Mexican War, he rejoined Sutter as a partner and began work on the sawmill project at a place known to the local Indians as Culumah on the South Fork of the American River. When Marshall found gold nuggets in the tail race of the mill on January 24, 1848, he was near completion of this project.

Both Marshall and Sutter made a vain attempt to keep the discovery of gold at Sutter's Mill a secret. Five workers Mormon workers, helping

Based on John Bigler's diary, the discovery of gold was established on Monday, Jan. 24, 1848. He refers to "some kind of mettle" found in the tail race.

John Bigler noted in his diary the discovery of "some kind of mettle" found in the tailrace. COURTESY JIM LENHOFF COLLECTION

125 years ago...

The first published account of James Marshall's discovery of gold at Coloma appeared in the state's first newspaper, the CALIFORNIAN, on March 15, 1848.

The account which follows was gathered together from over 20 sources. It originally appeared in California's oldest daily newspaper, the SACRAMENTO UNION, on January 21, 1973.

The first published account of James Marshall's discovery.
COURTESY JIM LENHOFF COLLECTION

Marshall build the mill, were present when he picked up the nuggets. Word of Marshall's discovery of gold soon spread to other Mormons building a flour mill for Sutter on the American River downriver from Sutter's Mill at a place called Mormon Island.

Some of the Mormons began to pan for gold, successfully, when they were not working on the mill. Sam Brannan, an Elder in the Mormon Church and the owner of the newspaper, The *California Star*, learned of the gold discovery from these workers. He soon visited Sutter's Mill and the even richer diggings at Mormon Island. Marshall's discovery went unnoticed for the most part until Brannan's entrepreneurial skills came into play. He set up stores at Sutter's Mill and Mormon Island in anticipation of the horde of miners who would soon arrive.

On May 12, 1848, Sam Brannan walked the streets of San Francisco, holding up a bottle filled with gold nuggets, and shouted, "Gold, gold, gold, from the American River." The streets of San Francisco were soon empty, as almost every citizen—some 800 in total—headed for the gold

James W. Marshall. COURTESY MARSHALL GOLD DISCOVERY STATE HISTORIC PARK

fields. James W. Marshall discovered the gold. Sam Brannan created the rush.

Those already in California were able to prospect for gold immediately. Only a few hundred people responded when word reached the east coast on April 15, 1848. The real rush began when President James K. Polk, in his annual message to Congress, wrote on December 5, 1848:

The accounts of abundance of gold are of such an extraordinary character, as would scarcely command belief were they not corroborated by the authentic reports of officers in the public service.

Gold fever swept the states and the world. The trickle of migrants to California turned to a rush in 1849 when an estimated 90,000 miners arrived in California. By land and by sea, miners rushed west to claim their share of wealth.

The 49ers (all who joined in the California Gold Rush were usually referred to as 49ers) came from Australia, Chile, China, England, France, Germany, Italy, Mexico, Panamá, Perú, the Sandwich Islands (Hawaii), and the States. The hordes of argonauts who roamed the gulches and canyons seeking the color dammed and virtually dug up the streambeds of all of the rivers and creeks in the Sierra Nevada.

Only a few 49ers found wealth mining for gold. Mining required standing all day in ice-cold water that flowed down from the High Sierra's melting snowpack, sifting tons of dirt in back breaking work while the hot California sun shone down from the bright blue sky. Many 49ers wrote in their diaries about long bouts with the "poison oak illness."

Few 49ers mined enough gold to provide for even a meager existence. Many 49ers "saw the elephant" and left penniless to return home. The majority of those made wealthy by the Gold Rush were merchants who sold food, supplies, and other services to the miners, usually at exorbitantly high prices. The two men associated with the discovery of gold at Sutter's Mill on January 24, 1848, did not profit. Marshall was given credit for discovery of gold at Coloma in the official government report prepared by Colonel Richard B. Mason but died a bitter and penniless man.

Hounded by gold seekers who thought that he possessed special powers, Marshall was unsuccessful in his quest to discover more gold in California's Gold Rush Country. He eventually returned to a small cabin on the hill above Coloma and worked as a carpenter for many years. Marshall sold souvenir name cards for 25 cents to help support himself. He died on August 10, 1885, at nearby Kelsey where he lived in a small room of the Union Hotel.

Marshall achieved recognition for his discovery of gold only after his death. A statue commemorating his discovery of gold was erected with much fanfare in 1890 at Coloma. In the role as "Boss of the Mill," Marshall found his place in world history.

Sutter, whose dream of New Helvetia was crushed by the rush of 49ers to the rivers and creeks on his lands, wrote in a letter to J. M. Hutchings, published in Hutchings' *California Magazine*, November 1857:

SUTTER'S MILL.

1848

Sutter's Mill.   COURTESY MARSHALL GOLD DISCOVERY STATE HISTORIC PARK

By this sudden discovery of the gold, all my great plans were destroyed. Had I succeeded with my mills and manufactories for a few years before the gold was discovered, I should have been the richest citizen on the Pacific shore; but had to be different. Instead of being rich, I am ruined.

The discovery of gold at Sutter's Mill and overextension of his operations led to Sutter's financial downfall. Prospectors occupied his lands and he was unable to evict them. Sutter then moved to his Hock Farm until he was forced from these lands by financial setbacks. From there, he moved to Lititz, Pennsylvania. He spent the balance of his life traveling to Washington, D.C., in vain attempts to petition Congress for restitution for his losses. Sutter, whose dreams of New Helvetia led to California's Gold Rush, died in 1880.

A number of men who participated in the Gold Rush used their findings or earnings to become successful businessmen, for example, Levi Strauss (Levi jeans), Studebaker (first wagons, then cars), Ghirardelli (chocolates), Crocker (banks and railroads), Macy (department stores), Stanford (University and railroads), Hearst (newspapers), and Chichizola (Bank of America).

DISCOVERY AND EARLY HISTORY OF CALIFORNIA

California first came to the attention of Europeans in 1542 when the Spanish explorer Juan Rodriguez Cabrillo sailed the length of its coast. He was followed by Sir Francis Drake in 1579, who claimed California for England. Sebastián Vizcaíno's voyages in the early 1600s resulted in the naming of most of the landmarks along the California coast.

When Spain became concerned about England's intentions in the area, Spain began land explorations of its own in 1769 that led to the colonization of Alta California. Presidios were established at the sea ports of San Francisco, Monterey, Santa Barbara, and San Diego, and pueblos (towns) at Los Angeles and San José. A chain of 21 missions, built a day's ride apart, extended from San Diego to Sonoma. The efforts of the Spanish led to the colonization and creation of an agricultural empire throughout Alta California. When Mexico achieved independence from Spain in 1821, the young nation encouraged agricultural pursuits in the region.

Early American explorers made their way west to California in the early 1800s. Their excursions into Alta California were generally peaceful. Most of these explorers were fur trappers, traders, scouts, and adventurers who became well known for their role in opening up the west to migration and permanent settlement. John Augustus Sutter, who arrived in California in 1839 and took Mexican citizenship, forged plans and dreams for a new empire, which he called New Helvetia, to be headquartered at Fort Sutter at the confluence of the American and Sacramento rivers. His personal dreams were ultimately shattered but the goal of western expansion for the United States were assured.

The way west from the United States to California began as a trickle in 1841. Thirty-two members of the Bidwell-Bartleson Party, led by John Bidwell, completed the first migration of pioneers whose purpose was to settle in California. While the Bear Flag Rebellion of 1846 led to control of California by General Stephen W. Kearny, the American military governor, it was only after news reached the east coast that gold was discovered at Sutter's Mill that migration west to California began in earnest. California became the 31st state on September 9, 1850.

POST GOLD RUSH

Much has changed from the days of the Gold Rush in California's Gold Rush Country. Little remains from the early years when "rush" truly characterized the miner's lifestyle. In their haste to find gold, the 49ers only took time to erect tents or simple cabins to provide basic shelter from the elements. On river bars and mountain sides where settlements sprang up and buildings erected, they were often destroyed by fire or collapsed from neglect after the 49ers "rushed" to another reported gold discovery.

The human mark on nature is still evident in many areas of California's Gold Rush Country after 150 years. Even though the several hundred thousand miners literally dug up all of the rivers and creeks in this area, little remains to mark the sites of hundreds of tent cities that sprang up along the banks and bars of creeks and rivers. Trees and brush have grown back over the banks of the streams. Subsequent floods have washed away many of the huge piles of rocks stacked up by the 49ers and restored the streambeds to their natural appearance.

Notable exceptions exist, of course, and none are more striking than the massive wastelands created at Malakoff Diggins in Nevada County, the Spring Valley Mine at Cherokee, and the La Grange Mine near Weaverville. Visitors to Columbia, Gem of the Southern Mines, can see acres of large rocks that protrude from the ground like silent, gray sentinels. These rocks, exposed by 49ers in their relentless search for gold, were once buried deep beneath the earth.

Hydraulic mining—which used huge nozzles, called monitors, to spray water on hillsides to wash away the dirt and gravel—was an effective and efficient way to uncover gold. However, this filled the adjacent rivers with mud, rocks and trees. The Yuba River filled with debris to a depth of 70 feet and forced the building of levees to protect Marysville. Hydraulic mining in California was virtually eliminated in 1884 by Judge Lorenzo in a court decision based on the Anti-Debris Act of 1883.

Estimates indicate that more than 600,000 men, women, and children made their way west to join in California's Gold Rush by 1858. Most came for the gold and returned home. Many of these people stayed on and helped develop California into the powerful economic force that eluded John Augustus Sutter.

Chapter Two

HOW TO USE THIS GUIDE

California's Gold Rush Country is spread over some 600 miles from Mariposa County in the Sierra Nevada to Humboldt County on the Pacific Ocean near the Oregon-California border. The best known area is along California Highway 49 (CA 49), which runs from Mariposa County north to Plumas County, a distance of 320 miles. Often referred to as the Mother Lode Country, the name is derived from the 100-mile-long vein of gold bearing quartz believed to be buried in the Sierra Nevada from Mariposa County to Nevada County.

California Highway 49—named in honor of the 49ers—runs through the heart of Gold Rush Country. Side roads lead to sites and places as exciting as those directly on CA 49. Even though its length can be driven in a single day, visitors will want to pick 1 or more segments to experience for a few days or take longer to visit the entire area.

The mining areas of California's Gold Rush Country are divided into the Southern Mines, those south of Auburn, and the Northern Mines, those located north of Auburn. *Traveling California's Gold Rush Country* begins at Coloma, where the Gold Rush began. From there, the guide moves from south to north along CA 49. The guide also covers Plumas County and Yuba County north and west to Humboldt County in northern California.

While visitors can readily find buildings and sites from the Gold Rush, little remains from the first few years. The "rush" was truly that, with few permanent buildings constructed. Camps and towns would rise virtually overnight on the news of a gold strike and disappear as quickly when the reported finds did not pan out or when claims there were

Route named in honor of the 49ers.

worked out. Because of this, the true flavor of the Gold Rush, the wild, rip-roaring camps of tents and thrown-together buildings, their "bawdy" houses, saloons, gambling halls and hotels, have vanished.

Of the sturdy permanent structures built during the "rush" of 1849 only a few have withstood the ravages of the elements, neglect, fire, and vandalism. These provide only a glimpse of what happened during the rush.

CALIFORNIA GOLD DISCOVERY TO STATEHOOD SESQUICENTENNIAL

From 1998 through 2000, California will commemorate the 150th anniversaries of the discovery of gold at Sutter's Mill (1848), the 49ers (1849) and Statehood (1850). In 1998, the theme will be California's Golden Discoveries (commemorating not just Marshall's discovery of gold but the "rushes" brought by Hollywood, oil, aerospace, and information technology). For 1999, the theme will be California's Rich Heritage (commemorating California's natural and cultural diversity). In 2000, the theme will focus on California's Statehood and Vision. These 3 years of activities will be an especially important time to visit because of the numerous related events scheduled in all areas of California.

SLEEPING WHERE PRESIDENTS, MARK TWAIN, BRET HARTE, AND 49ERS SLEPT

My current experience with California's Gold Rush Country began in May 1993 when I made the first of what became forty-six trips to research and prepare photography for a coffee table book project, *California's Gold Rush Country.*

I was surprised to discover that little from 1848, 1849, and 1850 remained and that most of those old buildings in my memory were mostly from the mid 1850s or even later. In time, I learned that flimsy construction, fire, vandalism, time, and the elements had taken a heavy toll on those early structures.

Fortunately, a number of historic structures remain to provide visitors with a fleeting glimpse of that early era. This guide concentrates on the most historic properties (both age and role). Most will be the "first," the "oldest," or the "longest continuously operating" because California's modern history originated with the Gold Rush.

Some of these structures are hotels where visitors can find overnight accommodations and food; some boast that Presidents, Mark Twain, Bret Harte, and other notables slept there. However, because of their limited size, they are usually able to accommodate only a small number of guests. Visitors who wish to make arrangements to stay in these properties should do as far in advance as possible to assure reservations. All recommendations are based on first-hand experience.

The City Hotel, Columbia State Historic Park.

Columbia State Historic Park.

There are many modern motels and hotels in California's Gold Rush Country that can accommodate large numbers of guests. These properties are not included in this guide but can be readily learned about from the tourist bureaus listed at the end of each chapter.

These tourist bureaus assist visitors with accommodations and general information about the area. During the spring and summer months, advance reservations are a must throughout the region. Because of the California Gold Discovery to Statehood Sesquicentennial, reservations will be a must throughout all areas of California.

THE CALIFORNIA HIGHWAY PATROL, 911, STOP SIGNS, GASOLINE, AND DEER

The California Highway Patrol and the various County Sheriff's Departments vigorously enforce rules of the highway, ever vigilant to speeders and those who drink to excess. Professional and courteous, these officers patrol the roads and highways of California Gold Rush Country to assure the safety of residents and tourists alike. Please drive safely.

In California's Gold Rush Country, and throughout California, dial "911" for all police, fire, and medical emergencies. Non-emergency numbers for police and fire department's can be obtained from local telephone directories or operators.

One of the most striking differences that a driver will notice while driving along CA 49 is that there are only 6 STOP signs from Oakhurst to Vinton, some 320 miles apart. There are 2 in Mariposa; 2 in Jackson; 1 in Cool north of San Andreas; and 1 at its northern terminus at Vinton. With the exception of the 20 or so in the urban sprawl area between Auburn and Grass Valley, there are only 3 other traffic signals on CA 49. The first is at its southern terminus in Oakhurst, the second at Sonora, and the third is at Altaville (just north of Jackson).

Gasoline and minor maintenance services are readily available in towns along the major roads throughout California's Gold Rush Country. Vehicle repair facilities are found in only a few towns, but unless you are in a remote area well off the beaten path, major repairs can be obtained with little inconvenience.

Deer are common in California's Gold Rush Country. "I swerved to avoid a deer" is ranked high as the cause of single-vehicle accidents. Watch for deer.

SEASONS AND TOPOGRAPHY

Seasons vary in California's Gold Rush Country. In the winter, rain falls at the lower elevations and snow falls in the higher elevations. The hillsides turn green during the short rainy season. Spring is usually brief but beautiful with fields of flowers almost everywhere in the Southern

Mines. Summer is long and hot; very hot (100 degrees Fahrenheit is common) and very dry, emphasized by the grasses withering and turning a golden hue. Fall is colorful—in the Northern Mines, with aspens in the mountains and maples imported by pioneer settlers coloring the towns and hillsides, and the hills of the Southern Mines covered in golden colored grasses.

The seasons vary with the topography of the area. The Northern Mines are generally much more mountainous, while the Southern Mines are made up of smaller, rounded hills covered with grass and pines. I have found that the scenery of California's Gold Rush Country is among the prettiest in the United States.

All visitors to California's Gold Rush Country must keep in mind that weather conditions in the Sierra Nevada can change rapidly. This is acutely so in the winter. The 49ers kept the infamous Donner Party Tragedy foremost in their mind as they traveled west, ever mindful that they must cross the Sierra Nevada before snows closed the trails. So, too, should the modern-day visitor, for the Donner Party Tragedy site is in California's Gold Rush Country. Even though CalTrans does an excellent job of keeping the major highways open during snow storms, travelers must exercise caution when driving in the Sierra Nevada during the winter.

A FEW CAVEATS ABOUT THIS GUIDE AND CALIFORNIA'S GOLD RUSH COUNTRY

Traveling California's Gold Rush Country is not a definitive guide to every site and stop in California's Gold Rush Country. This book provides a basic overview, which allows visitors to plan a trip (or trips) to discover the highlights of California's Gold Rush Country. Using information provided by this guide, visitors are encouraged to branch out on their own to find other, more current, attractions and scenic locales found throughout the region which may be of specific interest to them.

There are many "firsts" in California's Gold Rush Country. California's Gold Rush created towns overnight where none existed before and wagon roads were developed from former deer trails and Indian paths. Firsts are claimed by local civic pride for the "oldest building," "the oldest continuously operating business," etc. Because records were often lost in fires, these claims of "firsts" are often difficult to prove or, on the other hand, disprove.

PRIVATE PROPERTY AND POISON OAK

Two warnings should be heeded by those who visit California's Gold Rush Country; failure to do so can cause some uncomfortable consequences.

Much of the land in California's Gold Rush Country is privately owned. Obey all trespassing signs and posted mining claims. All of the sites written about in *Traveling California's Gold Rush Country* are open to the public.

I write from experience and suffering that poison oak (related, directly, to its eastern cousin, poison ivy) grows just about everywhere in California's Gold Rush Country. Remember, shiny leaves of 3, let them be! Because of the temperate weather in the Southern Mines area, some of the poison oak bushes grow like small trees. Indeed, diaries make note of the "poison oak illness" which laid up many an unwary 49er. For those who dare (or do not suffer the "poison oak illness"), each September the Poison Oak Festival is held at Columbia State Historic Park. I have skipped this event for obvious reasons.

SHOULD YOU DECIDE TO BECOME A MINER . . .

Should you decide that you want to mine for gold, here are a few helpful hints:

Keep in mind that you are unlikely to hit the big strike. The odds are stacked against you. The merchants made the most gold from the Gold Rush.

There are a number of casual panning sites in California's Gold Rush Country where you can spend a few hours trying your luck at panning. Panning operations at Rich Bar, Columbia State Historic Park, and Jamestown are mentioned in this guide.

Contact 1 of the many outfits in California's Gold Rush Country that specialize in 1- or 2-day guided gold-prospecting trips. Spend a day or 2 trying your luck in a creek or river before you strike out for the big time.

If you decide to go out on your own, there are a number of outfitters who will provide you with equipment and teach you how to find your fortune in gold. The Mother Lode is still out there, waiting to be discovered.

MINING TERMS

There are a number of types of mining and specialized words whose meaning you will need to know to better understand displays and conversations about gold mining while in California's Gold Rush Country.

Gold mining is a very labor intensive job. The individual miner dug up dirt that he believed contained gold. He usually put the gold bearing dirt in a bucket and took it to the edge of the creek or river where he was working. The miner would either put the dirt in a gold pan, cradle, long tom, or sluice. In many cases, miners worked in teams, sharing in the digging, carrying buckets of dirt and water, and operating the equipment to find gold.

Forty-niners operating a "long tom." COURTESY JIM LENHOFF COLLECTION

Each piece of equipment operated as follows:

Gold Pan: A special type of round, handle-less pan with a saucer-like shape that miners used to "pan for gold". The miner placed gold-bearing dirt in the pan, filled the pan with water, and moved the pan in a circular motion. The circular motion caused the dirt and water to wash over the side of the pan and the gold to settle to the bottom. After all of the dirt and water washed out of the pan, gold, if any, remained in the bottom of the pan. Forty-niners usually referred to the gold pan as a "wash bowl" or "wash pan."

Cradle (or Rocker): The cradle was an oblong box with a hopper on top. The miner placed gold-bearing dirt in the hopper, poured water over the hopper as he rocked the cradle from side to side. This action caused the dirt to wash over special bars, called riffles, in the bottom of the cradle. Gold was caught in the riffles and collected by the miners. This method was faster and more gold-bearing dirt could be processed than by using a pan.

Long Tom: The long tom was an improvement over the cradle. Gold-bearing dirt was placed on a riddle, a steel plate with holes, that allowed small pebbles and gold nuggets to fall through to riffles below where they were collected by the miners. The long tom was connected to a trough where water was continuously fed from the stream. The long tom was more efficient than the cradle.

Sluice: A more effective method of mining by teams of miners involved the sluice. In this operation, a series of riffle boxes were connected to a trough of continuously flowing water. This allowed more dirt to be processed than by using the cradle or long tom.

Other forms of mining required huge numbers of men, large amounts of equipment and huge sums of money to finance the operations. The most common methods were hydraulic mining and quartz mining.

Hydraulic Mining: The most efficient method developed for mining gold was hydraulic mining. Fed by canals and holding ponds, high pressure nozzles, called monitors, were used to wash away hills and mountains into sluices. This large-scale operation required large numbers of men to build canals, operate the monitors, and retrieve the gold. Although extremely efficient, hydraulic mining wreaked havoc on the environment. Sediment from the operations washed into the rivers, clogging them and causing flooding downstream. Hydraulic mining was restricted by the Anti-Debris Act of 1883. Excellent examples of hydraulic mining are the Malakoff Diggins State Historic Park and Cherokee.

Dredging: Dredging involved barges using huge buckets on conveyer belts which dug up river beds and deposited the gravel on a series of screens to process out the gold. Gold dredging was developed at Oroville

Hydraulic mining at Malakoff Diggins. COURTESY CALIFORNIA DEPARTMENT OF PARKS AND RECREATION

and a solitary gold dredger remains to be seen near La Grange in Stanislaus County.

Quartz Mining: Gold bearing quartz, formed when volcanic action melded gold and quartz, is usually found deep underground. Mining of gold bearing quartz required that ore be crushed in stamping mills and processed with mercury to remove the gold. Quartz mining museums are located at Jackson and Grass Valley.

Tailings: Residue from the crushed ore of quartz mining is called tailings.

ERRORS AND OMISSIONS

As you travel California's Gold Rush Country, if you find that information in this book is no longer accurate, or if there is an omission that you believe needs correction, please let us know so that we can update future editions of *Traveling California's Gold Rush Country*. Please write care of Falcon® Publishing, P.O. Box 1718, Helena, MT 59624 or e-mail to falcon@desktop.org.

Chapter Three

ORGANIZING YOUR TOUR OF CALIFORNIA'S GOLD RUSH COUNTRY

No matter what your level of experience as a traveler, you already know that you cannot see everything in the amount of time that you have allotted to your visit to California's Gold Rush Country. With so much to see, just what do you select to experience California's Gold Rush and what remains 150 years later? Obviously, to thoroughly experience California's Gold Rush requires weeks, months, or even longer. With so much to see, where do you drive to capture the essence of that era in the limited time that you have?

If you are the typical visitor, you have likely allowed 1, maybe 2 or perhaps even 3 days to take in California's Gold Rush Country as you drive from San Francisco, Reno, or Los Angeles to Yosemite or Lake Tahoe. *Traveling California's Gold Rush Country* is designed to allow you to plan your itinerary to suit the time that you have available. Your experience will depend on your point of entry to California's Gold Rush Country and your interests.

Sample itineraries outlined below will allow you to visit the more traveled areas of California's Gold Rush Country. Travel in the mountainous areas to a remote mining camp site can take hours each way on dirt roads. These trips are not recommended for those with a limited amount of time to spend in California's Gold Rush Country.

WHAT TO SEE IN CALIFORNIA'S GOLD RUSH COUNTRY

Exactly what you do or where you go is either your personal choice or limited by your available time. There are 2 mandatory sites to see, both only a few hours drive time apart. You should try to see both but visit at least 1 of the 2 sites. Marshall Gold Discovery State Historic Park at Coloma, site of Sutter's Mill, is the single most important site in California's Gold Rush Country. A walk along the riverbank in early morning fog to the site where James W. Marshall picked up the nuggets that led to the California Gold Rush can be a powerful experience for every visitor. The diaries of 49ers tell of their pilgrimages to where the Gold Rush all began, Sutter's Mill. So, too, should the modern day visitor go to the site of Sutter's Mill.

Columbia State Historic Park, site of Columbia, was one of the richest and most important gold mining towns during the era of California's Gold Rush. It is the only town preserved and operated as a Gold Rush town today. A walk along Main Street with its restored buildings and authentic shops is like stepping back in time. The clatter of horse hooves and creaking of a passing stagecoach create an ambiance of earlier days.

TOURING CALIFORNIA'S GOLD RUSH COUNTRY IN 1 DAY ON HIGHWAY 49

If there is just 1 day for you to experience California's Gold Rush Country, you can drive from Mariposa to Nevada City, or the reverse, with 1 hour stops at Marshall Gold Discovery State Historic Park and Columbia State Historic Park. Historic districts for all of the towns along the way, with the exceptions of Jamestown, San Andreas, Jackson, Placerville, Auburn, and Grass Valley, are directly on Highway 49. Drive time plus lunch and a few stretch breaks will take about 8 hours.

TOURING CALIFORNIA'S GOLD RUSH COUNTRY IN 2 DAYS ON HIGHWAY 49

With 2 days to drive Highway 49 from Mariposa to Nevada City, not only can you make the required visits to Marshall Gold Discovery State Historic Park and Columbia State Historic Park, you will be able to stop and sample the essence of California's Gold Rush Country. Plan on walking tours in the historic districts of Mariposa, Jamestown, Sonora, Angels Camp, San Andreas, Mokelumne Hill, Jackson, Sutters Creek, Murphys, Placerville (a.k.a. Hangtown), Auburn, Grass Valley, and Nevada City. Museum stops should include the Mariposa Museum and History Center, the Amador County Museum in Jackson, the Shenandoah Valley Museum east of Plymouth, the Courthouse Museum in Auburn and the Empire Mine State Historic Park in Grass Valley. Placerville, Sutter Creek or Jackson make good midpoint towns to stay overnight on this schedule.

ONE/TWO DAY TOUR OF CA 49

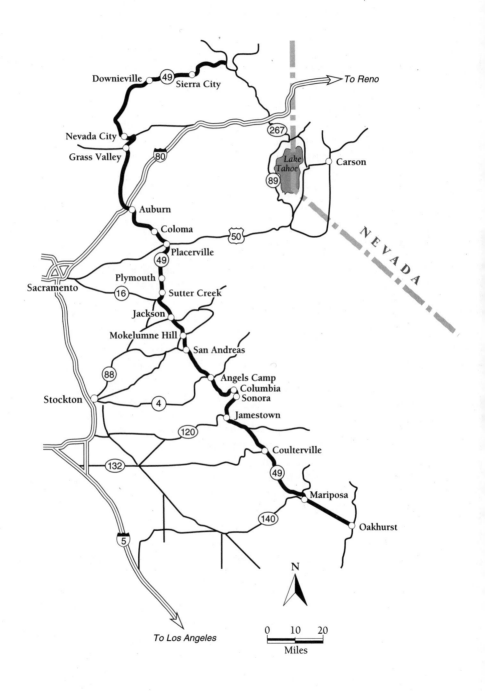

TOURING THE NORTHERN MINES IN 1 DAY

The most scenic areas in California's Gold Rush Country are found in the Northern Mines area, those north and east of Auburn. Because of the hills and curves and rivers and mountains to cross, driving time is much slower but the scenery is grand. Visitors can easily spend days in this area and not see everything. A 1 day sampler tour on the main roads through the area will allow you to get a good idea, however. Please note that the suggested drive will take 10 to 12 hours. This driving route is best seen in 2 days if time permits.

The suggested starting point can be either Sacramento, Marysville or, even better, Oroville. Time your arrival in the Feather River Gorge after 9 A.M. for the best daylight and best views. The Feather River National Scenic Byway begins about 10 miles north of Oroville. For the next 30 miles, CA 70 winds along beside the North Branch of the Feather River with spectacular vistas at each turn in the road. There are numerous places to stop and take in the magnificent scenery and contemplate the difficulty which the 49ers experienced as they traveled through the Feather River Canyon.

Stop at Rich Bar for an hour. Purchase a bucket of dirt from Norm Grant, the owner, or dig your own, and pan for gold. Norm will be happy to fill you in on the rich history of this small river bar. Besides being the richest river bar in all of California's Gold Rush Country, Rich Bar was the home of Dame Shirley, the wife of a doctor who spent a year here during the Gold Rush. Her numerous letters home have proved to be historically significant for their exquisite detail about life—and death—in the mining camp established on this small bar in the bend of the Feather River.

Continue to Quincy and, at Graeagle, turn south on Gold Lake Road and drive through the Sierra Lakes Basin to CA 49. This road is open from April until November, when deep snow blankets the area. Pause at Gold Lake to contemplate the scene in 1850 when several thousand miners showed up here expecting to find gold nuggets the size of their fists. On Gold Lake Road, you will get your first glimpse of the Sierra Buttes.

At CA 49, turn south to Sierra City, located below the peaks of the Sierra Buttes. Follow the Yuba River to Downieville, a town rich in Gold Rush buildings and set in 1 of the most picturesque settings in all of California's Gold Rush Country. Take time to stroll Main Street and its Gold Rush buildings. The road south on CA 49 passes through the spectacular canyon of the Yuba River making this area the prettiest drive on CA 49. Follow CA 49 south to Nevada City.

If you have 2 days for this route, include stops at the Cherokee Museum north of Oroville, the Plumas County Museum in Quincy, the Plumas Eureka State Park at Blairsden, the Kentucky Mine Museum at Sierra City, and consider a trip to the Alleghany Mining Museum, high on the Pliocene Ridge between the Middle Fork and the North Fork of

NORTHERN MINES—ONE DAY

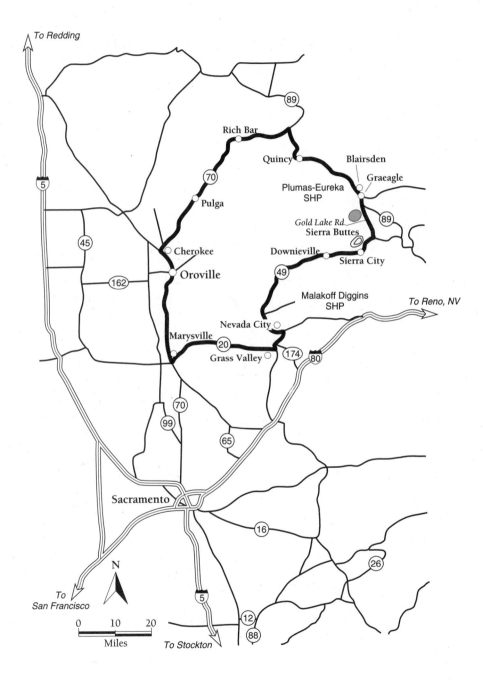

the Yuba River, and to Malakoff Diggins State Historic Park where miners washed away a mountain of dirt to get to rich gravel bearing gold. Quincy, Graeagle, Sierra City, or Downieville are good places to stay overnight. Advance reservations are suggested.

TOURING THE NORTHERN MINES OF SHASTA AND TRINITY COUNTIES

Important mining centers were located in Shasta and Trinity counties in northern California near Redding. Perhaps overlooked because they are in a remote and less traveled area of California, they are important historic sites and the Trinity River Canyon is as wild and scenic as any in the Northern Mines. The drive from Redding to Arcata, with stops, will take most of a day due to the winding road through the Trinity River Canyon. CA 299 has been designated as the Trinity Scenic Byway from Shasta to Blue Lake, and the Trinity River has been designated as the Wild and Scenic Trinity River.

SHASTA/TRINITY

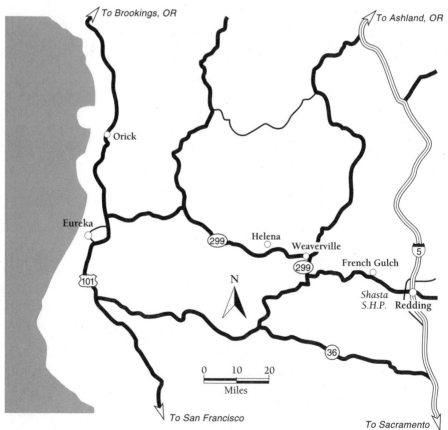

SHASTA/TRINITY DETAIL A

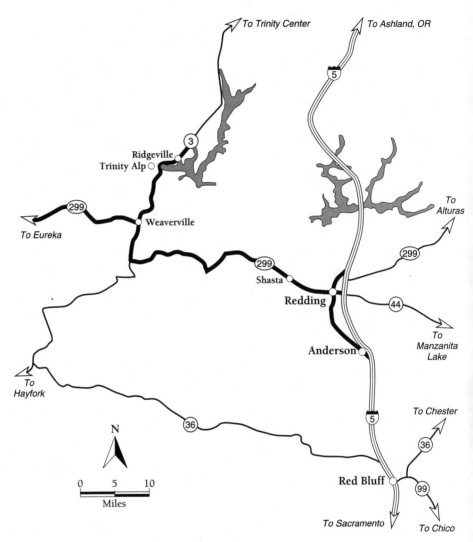

To Trinity Center

To Ashland, OR

⑤

Ridgeville
Trinity Alp ○
③

To Alturas

②⑨⑨
Weaverville

To Eureka

②⑨⑨
Shasta ○

②⑨⑨

Redding

④④

Anderson

To Manzanita Lake

To Hayfork

③⑥

⑤

To Chester

③⑥

N

Red Bluff

⑨⑨

0 5 10
Miles

To Sacramento

To Chico

Redding is located 165 miles north of Sacramento on I-5. Drive west on CA 299 to Shasta State Historic Park, take a side trip to French Gulch, and plan on an hour or more in the historic district of downtown Weaverville. Especially scenic with the Trinity Alps in the background, Weaverville has 1 of 3 well-preserved Chinese Joss Houses in California's Gold Rush Country. Several buildings on Main Street have spiral staircases to the upper levels. The drive from Weaverville along the Wild and Scenic Trinity River to Helena and Burnt Ranch is memorable for its scenic beauty.

TOURING CALIFORNIA'S GOLD RUSH COUNTRY FROM SAN FRANCISCO, SACRAMENTO, RENO, YOSEMITE NATIONAL PARK AND LOS ANGELES.

You can conveniently begin or end your tours of California's Gold Rush Country from San Francisco, Sacramento, Reno, Yosemite National Park, and Los Angeles. Take I-80, from San Francisco (120 miles), Sacramento (30 miles), and Reno (100 miles), to CA 49 at Auburn. Coloma is 25 miles south and Nevada City is 25 miles north of Auburn.

Yosemite National Park is in Mariposa County near the southern end of CA 49 and about 1 hour from Mariposa. The drive from Los Angeles to Mariposa takes 5 hours; Sonora is only 6 hours away from Los Angeles via I-5 and CA 99.

SHASTA/TRINITY DETAIL B

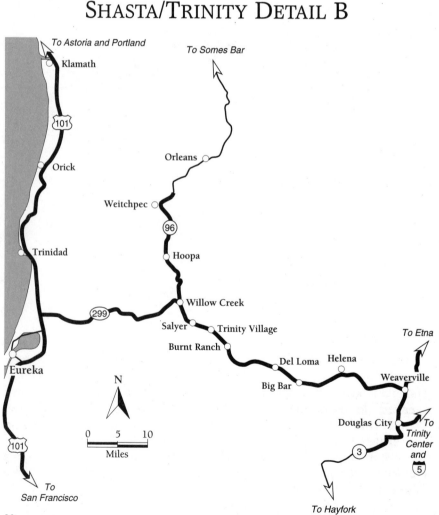

TOURING ALL OF CALIFORNIA'S GOLD RUSH COUNTRY

If you are fortunate enough to have 1 or more weeks to tour California's Gold Rush Country, you will be able to see just about all of the historic sites on CA 49, the Northern Mines including Shasta and Trinity counties, and Bodie State Historic Park, the most famous of the California Ghost Towns.

For a guide to all of California's Gold Rush Country, call the California Division of Tourism at 800-GO-CALIF (800-462-2543).

Chapter Four

SUTTER'S MILL: WHERE THE GOLD RUSH BEGAN

The site of Sutter's Mill at Marshall Gold Discovery State Historic Park in Coloma is usually a quiet and tranquil place. The tranquillity of the valley and the river today belies the events that followed James Marshall's discovery of gold on the North Bank of the South Fork of the American River.

Besieged by thousands of miners after Marshall's discovery of nuggets in the tail race of Sutter's Mill, the area was quickly mined out and the miners moved on to other areas. Thousands of 49ers continued to come to the site out of curiosity. They wanted to see where the Gold Rush began. Some 49ers believed that a visit to Marshall's gold discovery site would bring them good luck in the gold fields of the Sierra Nevada.

Just like the 49ers, visitors still come today to see what remains at Coloma and to say that they have been to where the Gold Rush began. A visit to Coloma is a must for a complete perspective of the California Gold Rush.

The sites of Marshall's discovery and of Coloma and its remaining historic buildings have been incorporated into the 143-acre Marshall Gold Discovery State Historic Park. Roads, trails, and footpaths provide visitors with easy access to all areas of the gold discovery area.

Coloma was founded in 1850. Its name was taken from the word Culumah, which the local Indians called this area along the American River.

Only a few buildings remain from early Coloma. The Wah Hop Building and the Man Lee Store were built to serve the large Chinese population. Bekeart's Gunshop (1854), built by Frank Bekeart, is the 3rd

U.S. National Gold-panning Championships at Coloma. Panning contestant signals that he has found all of the gold in his bucket of dirt.

MARSHALL GOLD DISCOVERY
STATE HISTORIC PARK

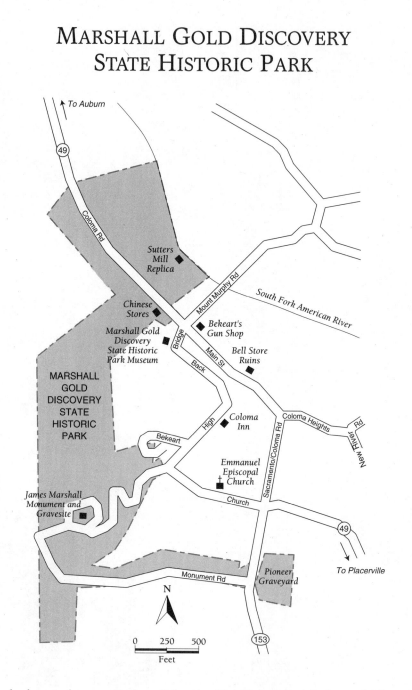

To Auburn

49

Coloma Rd

Sutters
Mill
Replica

Mount Murphy Rd

South Fork American River

Chinese
Stores

Bekeart's
Gun Shop

Marshall Gold
Discovery
State Historic
Park Museum

Bridge

Main St

Bell Store
Ruins

Back

MARSHALL
GOLD
DISCOVERY
STATE
HISTORIC
PARK

High

Coloma
Inn

Coloma Heights

Rd

Bekeart

Sacramento/Coloma Rd

New River

Emmanuel
Episcopal
Church

James Marshall
Monument and
Gravesite

Church

49

To Placerville

Monument Rd

Pioneer
Graveyard

N

0   250   500

Feet

153

such shop to be operated on this site. The Emmanuel Episcopal Church
(1856) is the largest building in Coloma. The nearby Coloma County Inn
(1852) was built as a residence. The Bell Store (1858) is now in ruins. The
I.O.O.F. Hall (1854) continues to serve as a community hall.

The replica of Sutter's Mill, constructed in 1967 near the site of the original, dominates the setting on the east side of CA 49. Adjacent to the mill replica is a replica of the Mormon Cabin used by workers who helped build Sutter's Mill. The exact spot where Marshall picked up the nuggets that brought gold seekers to this valley and to all of the Sierra Nevada is 100 yards downriver.

Across CA 49 on the west side is the Marshall Gold Discovery State Historic Park Museum. Here, exhibits explain the history of Sutter's Mill and displays from archeological digs in 1924 show timbers recovered from the original mill. The grounds around the Museum feature displays of old freight wagons, mining equipment, bedrock mortars used by Indians to grind acorns, and an old jail cell from the El Dorado County Jail House. The Pioneer Cemetery is at the southern edge of the park.

When James W. Marshall died on August 10, 1885, he was buried on the hill overlooking the site where he first discovered gold. The monument commemorating this event stands on the site of his grave on the hill above Coloma. The fingers of his right hand point down to the exact spot on the banks of the American River where his discovery of gold led to the greatest rush of humanity in the history of the United States. The trail and the road to the top of the hill both pass the Marshall Cabin.

VISITING MARSHALL GOLD DISCOVERY STATE HISTORIC PARK

Marshall Gold Discovery State Historic Park is on CA 49 about 8 miles north of Placerville and 28 miles south of Auburn. Marshall Gold Discovery State Historic Park is a compact park with easy walking access through streets, trails and pathways to all areas except for the James W. Marshall Monument on the hill above Coloma. The Monument can be reached via a well maintained but steep trail or driven to on a paved access road. A recreational gold panning site is on the east side of American River near the bridge.

A number of events take place each year at Marshall Gold Discovery State Historic Park. Each January 24th, Marshall's discovery of gold on the site is commemorated with special activities. The 1998 event, on the sesquicentennial of the discovery of gold is certain to be especially memorable. Coloma is the site of the US National Gold Panning Championships the first weekend of October. In 1998, the World Gold Panning Championships and Gold Rush Week with be celebrated from September 28 through October 4. Contestants are expected from all over the world, just as in the Gold Rush. For additional information about these and other scheduled events, call 916 622-3470.

Marshall Gold Discovery State Historic Park is open daily during daylight hours. Museum hours: Daily, 10 A.M. to 5 P.M. Fee: $5 per vehicle. Marshall Gold Discovery State Historic Park, 310 Back Street, P.O. Box 265, Coloma, CA 95613; 916-622-3470.

Marshall Gold Discovery State Historic Park.

For reservations at the Coloma Country Inn (1854), 345 High Street, P.O. Box 502, Coloma, CA 95613; 916-621-6919. The Sutter's Mill replica is 0.4 mile away.

Coloma County Inn (1854).

Chapter Five

MARIPOSA COUNTY

Mariposa County, originally established in 1850, was once the largest county ever created in the United States. Before being carved up to created an additional 11 counties, Mariposa County covered one-fifth of California. Mariposa, with just 17,000 residents, is sparsely populated. The only incorporated town, Hornitos, has just 75 residents. Mariposa Country is perhaps been known as the western gateway to Yosemite National Park and much of the park is within the county. Mariposa means "butterfly" in Spanish. Mariposa County is a beautiful area of California's Gold Rush Country, especially in the spring when wildflowers cover the hills and butterflies fill the air.

Mariposa is an excellent place to stay overnight at the beginning or ending of your tour of California's Gold Rush Country. There are a number of modern hotels, motels, bed and breakfast inns, RV facilities, and restaurants in Mariposa.

MARIPOSA

The Mariposa County Courthouse (1854), distinguished as the oldest courthouse west of the Mississippi in continuous use, is a striking example of Gold Rush architecture and one of the most important of those remaining Gold Rush era buildings in California's Gold Rush Country. Mariposa County Courthouse, on Bullion Street, has been the site of important jury decisions that have determined much of the law that governs mining operations in the western United States today.

Mariposa Overview

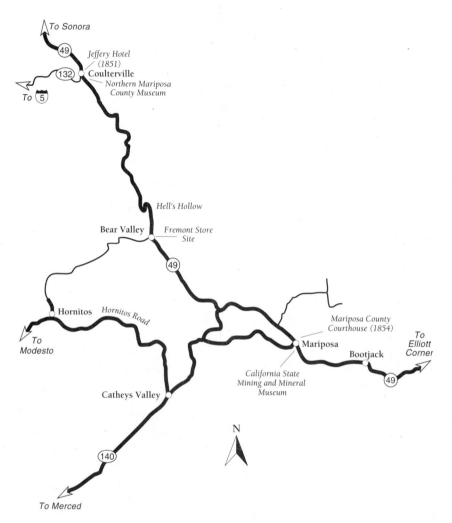

To Sonora

(49)

Jeffery Hotel
(1851)

(132) Coulterville

Northern Mariposa
County Museum

To (5)

Hell's Hollow

Bear Valley

Fremont Store
Site

(49)

Hornitos   Hornitos Road

To
Modesto

Mariposa County
Courthouse (1854)

To
Elliott
Corner

Mariposa

Bootjack

California State
Mining and Mineral
Museum

(49)

Catheys Valley

N

(140)

To Merced

The Fremont case is perhaps one of the most important. General John C. Fremont bought a "floating land grant" in 1849 and set up headquarters in nearby Bear Valley. When gold was discovered on his lands, he "floated" the boundaries to include most of the gold fields in the area. His claims were challenged in one of the landmark cases regarding mining claims. Fremont prevailed in a case argued in this room in 1856.

One of the striking features of the courtroom is its simplicity. The old wood-burning stove dominates the center of the room. The hand-hewn judge's bench is the same one used since 1854. The only apparent concession for modern usage of the courtroom is the computer terminal on the Clerk of the Court's desk.

MARIPOSA

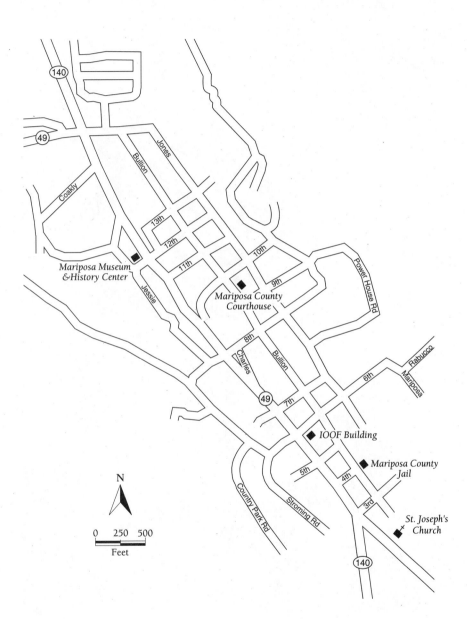

Mariposa Museum
&History Center

Mariposa County
Courthouse

IOOF Building

Mariposa County
Jail

St. Joseph's
Church

N

0   250   500
Feet

Mariposa Museum and History Center.

When the cupola and clock were added in 1866, the local newspaper, The Mariposa Gazette predicted problems.

> It will be a very extra affair, the courthouse ain't fenced in and how unfortunate if some of the scores of hogs that have their nests around there, should poke their nose under the corners and shake the pendulum off the time.

So far, that dire prediction made by *The Mariposa Gazette*, first published in 1854 and the second oldest newspaper in California's Gold Rush Country, has not come true.

Because the Mariposa County Courthouse is in active use during weekdays 8 A.M. to 5 P.M., the courtroom is not open to visitors when court is in session. Mariposa County Courthouse, Bullion Street between 9th and 10th Streets. Hours: 10 A.M. to 5 P.M., weekends May through September.

Other historic buildings in Mariposa are the I.O.O.F. building (1866), still used for local events, the abandoned Trabucco Warehouse (1866) and the Schlageter Hotel (1866) now used to house retail outlets. All are on Main Street and were built after the second disastrous fire destroyed much of Mariposa in 1866. St. Joseph's Church (1861) stands majestically on a knoll beside CA 49 at the southern entrance to Mariposa.

For an excellent perspective on gold mining throughout California's Gold Rush Country, take time to tour the Mariposa Museum & History Center and the California State Mining and Mineral Museum. After touring these facilities, you will have the necessary knowledge to see and understand what the Gold Rush era was all about.

The Mariposa Museum & History Center has displays which include a 5-stamp mill, a typical 1-room miner's cabin and much information about John C. Fremont, who played a major role in opening up the west, establishing statehood for California and contributing to the development of Mariposa County.

The Mariposa Museum & History Center, 5119 Jessie Street, P.O. Box 606, Mariposa, CA 95338; 209-966-2924. Hours: Seasonal, February, March, November, and December, weekends from 10 A.M. to 4 P.M.; April through October, open daily, 10 A.M. to 4:30 P.M. Entry is free; donations welcomed.

The California State Mining and Mineral Museum (Mariposa County Fairgrounds, 1.8 miles south of central Mariposa on CA 49) houses the official California collection of gold, gems, and minerals. Besides displays of mining artifacts and gold pieces, there is a 200-foot-deep mine tunnel. The California State Mining and Mineral Museum is open seasonally. Hours: May 1 through September 30, Wednesday through Monday, 10 A.M. to 6 P.M., and October 1 through April 30, Wednesday through Sunday, 10 A.M. to 4 P.M. Admission: Adults $3.50; Students and Seniors

$2.50; under fourteen, free. P.O. Box 1192, Mariposa, CA 95338; 209-742-7625.

TOURING MARIPOSA

Mariposa's central district has been designated as a historic district. The Mariposa County Courthouse, the farthest historic site from the southern entrance of Mariposa, is about 0.75 mile from St. Joseph's Church. Take time to walk up Bullion Street to the Mariposa Jail (between 4th and 5th Street), go 1 block down Fifth Street to CA 49 and the Schlageter Hotel and the I.O.O.F., both buildings on the same block, up CA 49 to 12th Street to the Mariposa County History Center and Museum. Allow at least an hour to see the extensive exhibits here. From the Museum, either drive or walk up 12th Street to Bullion Street and south to the Mariposa County Courthouse.

The Meadow Creek Ranch bed and breakfast (1858) is located 11 miles south of Mariposa off CA 49 on 2669 Triangle Road. The house is a beautifully restored stage station with attractive grounds; 209-966-3843.

After touring Mariposa, head west for Hornitos. Drive south on CA 140 to Cathey's Valley, turn right (or north) on Hornitos Road. Drive to Hornitos and turn right on Bear Valley Road. This takes you the 0.25 mile into the center of Hornitos.

HORNITOS

During the Gold Rush, Hornitos and its neighbor, Quartzburg, held the dubious distinction for being the richest and the roughest towns in California's Gold Rush Country. The notorious Mexican Bandit Joaquin Murieta reportedly visited Hornitos frequently. Despite the fact that Hornitos once had a population of 15,000 people and 12 hotels, 36 saloons and brothels, there are only 75 residents in Hornitos today.

There is just 1 business establishment, the Plaza Bar, in a building that dates to the 1860s. Numerous publications report bullet holes exist in the frame of its entrance door. I could not find any and the owner, Manuela Ortiz, disclaims knowledge of any. The town plaza was reportedly patterned after those in Sonora, Mexico. Hornitos was settled by Mexicans from Sonora.

Unlike its rowdy past, Hornitos is quiet, something that its residents think is just great. All of the buildings in Hornitos are private so please keep this in mind while looking around the town.

Hornitos' most famous building, the Ghirardelli Store, now in ruins is just across the street from the plaza. Domingo Ghirardelli arrived at Hornitos in 1849 and moved on to San Francisco in 1855 with his now world-famous chocolates. The Wells, Fargo & Company building ruin is a hundred yards south of the plaza. The Gagliardo Building (1852 or 1853)

HORNITOS

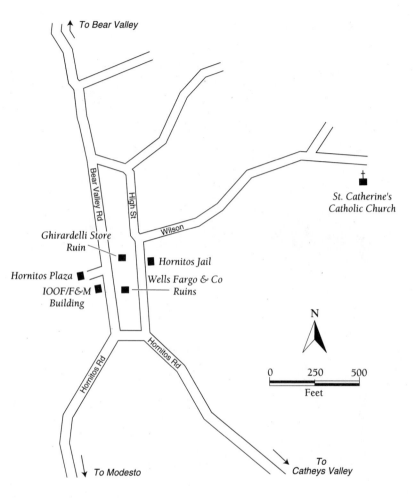

To Bear Valley

Bear Valley Rd

High St

Wilson

Ghirardelli Store
Ruin

Hornitos Plaza

IOOF/F&M
Building

Hornitos Jail

Wells Fargo & Co
Ruins

St. Catherine's
Catholic Church

Hornitos Rd

Hornitos Rd

To Modesto

To
Catheys Valley

N

0   250   500
Feet

is north of the plaza about 0.1 mile. Above the plaza, on High Street, is the Hornitos Jail (1849), the oldest remaining structure in Hornitos. It is a very small 1-room building. Confinement in the tiny structure could not have been pleasant.

From the plaza, you can literally see everything except the St. Catherine's Church (1869) above town on the crest of a hill. After visiting the sites of lower Hornitos, drive up Church Street to St. Catherine's Church. The most interesting features here are the ruins of several small brick oven-like ("hornitos") grave markers about 100 yards directly behind the church. They are believed to have originated with the Sonorans who established Hornitos.

Meadow Creek Ranch bed and breakfast.

Other than the Plaza Bar, there are no services in Hornitos. After completing your tour here, continue on to Bear Valley by driving north from Hornitos on the Bear Valley Road (the only road leading north from Hornitos). After reaching CA 49, turn right for 0.25 mile to the center of Bear Valley. Park on the east side of CA 49 across from the Oso Museum and the Simpson & Trabucco Store (the latter has a gas pump in front).

BEAR VALLEY

Most of Bear Valley's historic buildings are in ruins. Bear Valley was established by General John C. Fremont who bought a "floating land grant" in 1849 for $3,000. Named Rancho Las Mariposas, the ranch consisted of 44,000 acres and was headquartered in Bear Valley. When gold was discovered on his lands, Fremont "floated" the boundaries to include most of the gold fields in the area. He won a court battle when his claims were challenged in a case argued in the nearby Mariposa County Courthouse. Fremont sold his land holdings for 6 million dollars by 1860.

After parking, and before walking across to the Simpson & Trabucco Store, look south. From this vantage point, you can see all that remains of historic Bear Valley. Cross CA 49 to the west side to the Simpson & Trabucco Store. Owned by a descendant of the Trabucco family, this business has operated continuously since 1850 and is the oldest in Mariposa County. The store is the oldest continuously operating grocery store/gas/deli in the California Gold Rush Country owned by the same family.

40

Gagliardo Store Ruins.

For a short tour of Bear Valley, from the Simpson & Trabucco Store, walk 100 yards south to the Bon Ton Café (1860) on the west side of CA 49. This establishment has served as saloon and Wells, Fargo & Company office and last served as a restaurant. Across (east side) CA 49 and slightly south are the fast disappearing ruins of the Gagliardo Store (early 1850s).

About 50 yards south of the Bon Ton Café, on the west side of CA 49, are the crumbling walls of the Frémont Store (early 1850s). To the north and adjacent to the Bon Ton Cafe is the roofless stone building which housed the offices of the Mariposa Mining Company. Across from the Bon Ton Café (in the vicinity of where you parked) is the site of the Oso Hotel, a major landmark that was destroyed by fire in 1937.

Stop in at the Simpson & Trabucco Store. If the clerk on duty has time, he or she will close up the store and take you next door to the Oso Museum which houses artifacts of the Gold Rush. The Simpson & Trabucco Store, 7313 Highway 49, Bear Valley, CA. Hours: 9 A.M. to 7 P.M., daily; 209-377-8424.

Drive north on CA 49 for 2 miles. At the top of the hill, as the road turns right, slow down and turn left into a parking area. Walk to the stone wall and peer over. Below you is Hell's Hollow, 1 of the most impressive sights on CA 49. A thousand feet down and a mile away is Lake McClure, the result of damming the Merced River. After enjoying the view, drive down the hill to Lake McClure. There are several pulloffs to contemplate the beauty of the area once you reach the north side of the bridge.

The view of Hell's Hollow is one of the most impressive views on CA 49.

Proceed to Coulterville 13 miles north on CA 49. In the springtime, wildflowers cover the hills in this area.

COULTERVILLE

The Jeffery Hotel (1851) dominates the view of the town center at the intersection of CA 49 and CA 132. The hotel, the oldest building in Coulterville, clearly shows the influence of its Mexican heritage. The hotel has changed little since its construction in 1851, with the exception of bathrooms, electricity, and the television set in the bar. Teddy Roosevelt, King Kiahaumiahoea of Hawaii, Carry Nation (the prohibitionist), Frank James (the bandit), John D. Rockefeller (the financier), and John Muir (the preservationist) are among the notables who have slept in the Jeffery Hotel. The Magnolia Saloon, with its large bar, looks like a setting right out of the Gold Rush days, which is the case, of course. For reservations, call 209-878-3471 or (800) 464-3471.

The entire town of Coulterville, founded in 1850 by George W. Coulter, has been designated as a State Historical Landmark. At one time, there were 25 saloons, 10 hotels and more than 5,000 residents. The Northern Mariposa County History Center, across CA 49 from the Jeffery Hotel, is housed in the ruins of the Coulterville Hotel, the Wells, Fargo & Company building (1856), and McCarthy's Store. Nelson T. Cody, brother of "Buffalo Bill" Cody, served as agent and postmaster

The Jeffery Hotel.

Whistling Billy.

here from 1866 to 1876. Excellent exhibits highlight the area pioneer and Gold Rush heritage. Whistling Billy, a narrow gauge engine that was shipped around Cape Horn in 1897 for use in the nearby Mary Harrison Mine, is located under Coulterville's "hangin' tree" at the edge of CA 49. The museum is open seasonally; April through October, 10 A.M. to 4 P.M., closed Mondays; November through March, 10 A.M. to 4 P.M., Thursday through Sunday. Closed for the month of January; 209-878-3074.

From the museum, cross back to the east side of CA 49 and drive up Main Street (referred to on some maps as Greeley Hill Road). Historic structures are located on both sides of the street including the Gazzola Building and the I.O.O.F. building. At the top of the hill, on the right, is the Sun Sun Wo Store (1851). It is one of the best preserved Chinese structures in California's Gold Rush Country. The building is closed to the public.

After you have completed your tour of Coulterville, continue north on CA 49 for 12 miles through rolling hills and sharp curves to Moccasin Creek or consider side trips to Yosemite, Ben Hur, or LaGrange.

COULTERVILLE

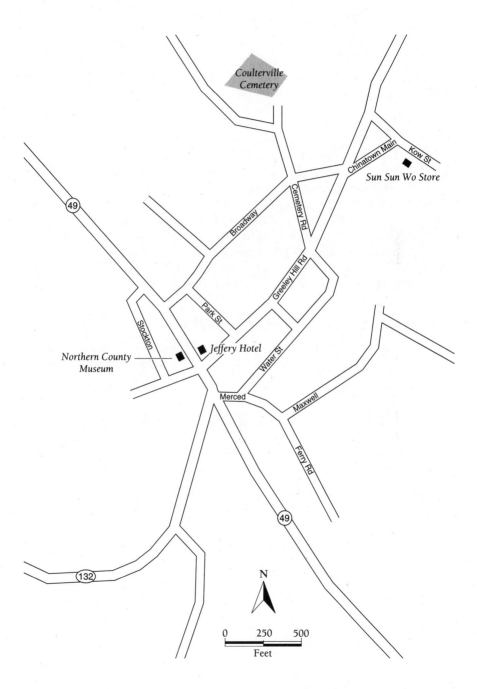

Coulterville Cemetery

Chinatown Main

Kow St

Sun Sun Wo Store

Cemetery Rd

Broadway

Greeley Hill Rd

49

Park St

Stockton

Northern County Museum

Jeffery Hotel

Water St

Merced

Maxwell

Ferry Rd

49

132

N

0   250   500
Feet

MARIPOSA COUNTY SIDE TRIPS

YOSEMITE NATIONAL PARK

If you plan to visit Yosemite National Park, the park can be reached via Highway 140 from Mariposa or via Highway J132, the first highway into Yosemite, from Coulterville. Either drive is scenic with rewarding vistas at almost every turn of the highway.

BEN HUR

For those with time, a drive in the countryside south and west of Mariposa to the community of Ben Hur is very rewarding, particularly in the spring when flowers are at their prettiest. From Mariposa, go south on CA 49 to Ben Hur Road, across from the Mariposa County Fairgrounds (also California's State Mining and Mineral Museum). Go west about 15 miles. At Ben Hur, on the south side of the highway, there is an old stone fence (1862), some 5 miles in length, built for the Quick Ranch (1859) by Chinese laborers. The rolling hills and gushing creeks create a scenic delight in the springtime. Return to Mariposa by the same route.

LAGRANGE (STANISLAUS COUNTY)

See LaGrange, Stanislaus County, for information about the only gold dredger in California's Gold Rush Country that is available to the public.

MARIPOSA COUNTY TRAVEL INFORMATION

MARIPOSA COUNTY CHAMBER OF COMMERCE
Telephone: 800-208-2434 or 209-966-2456; FAX 209-742-5409.
Mailing Address: P.O. Box 425, Mariposa, CA 95338.
Street Address: 5158 highway 140.
Internet Address: http//www.yosemite.net/mariposa/visitor
E-mail: visitor@yosemite.net.

Chapter Six

STANISLAUS COUNTY

This county had a pivotal role as a supply center and was much less known for mining activity. A number of interesting landmarks and sites are close to CA 49, however, and provide opportunity for interesting side trips.

LAGRANGE

Located at the intersection of CA 132 and CA 59, LaGrange is easily reached from Coulterville via CA 132, a distance of 24 miles through beautiful hills and around manmade lakes. One of 2 remaining gold dredgers—and the only one visitors can see—used in the early twentieth century to remove all possible remaining gold from the riverbeds in California's Gold Rush Country is here at LaGrange. The other, near Marysville in Yuba County, is not accessible to visitors. If you want to see a gold dredger, this is your only opportunity.

Approaching LaGrange from Coulterville, the first building on the right is the Inman Building (1850-1851), which houses the LaGrange Museum. Located at 31068 Yosemite Boulevard, the museum is open from 11 A.M. to 3 P.M. on Sundays, only, from April through October (and sometimes November). Mailing Address: P.O. Box 173, LaGrange, CA 95329; 209-853-2112.

The gold dredger can be visited by driving west on CA 132 for 0.5 mile west to the intersection of CA 59. Turn south (left) and drive 1 mile. As you round the second curve, on the right, there is a small road with a

STANISLAUS COUNTY

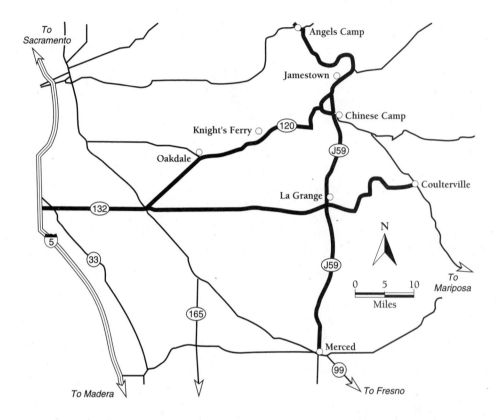

gate which leads to a field owned by the Stanislaus County Parks & Recreation Commission.

Park your vehicle here and walk through the small passageway for 0.25 mile straight ahead to the rusting hulk of the gold dredger. Do not attempt to climb on the gold dredger as its condition is, at best, deteriorating. The gold dredger has been in this pond since 1946 and seems destined to simply rust in place. One of its huge buckets is displayed in front of the LaGrange Museum.

After completing your tour of LaGrange, return via CA 132 to CA 49 in Coulterville. Or, if you prefer, you can reach Knight's Ferry, the other site of historic interest in Stanislaus County, by driving north on CA 59 to CA 120 and then west. Return to CA 49 to continue your tour north. Knight's Ferry can be easily reached from Chinese Camp on CA 120.

Rafters put in the Stanislaus just below the Knight's Ferry Covered Bridge.

KNIGHT'S FERRY

Knight's Ferry was an important river crossing on the road from Stockton to Sonora and the Southern Mines. A ferry operated here as early as 1850, shuttling traffic across the Stanislaus River. The first Knight's Ferry Covered Bridge was built in 1854. It was designed by then Army Captain Ulysses S. Grant, who was in Knight's Ferry to visit his sister. That bridge washed away in the flood of 1862. The current bridge, built in 1864 as a replica of the first bridge, is the longest covered bridge in the west. It is 330 feet long. The bridge is now open only to foot traffic.

An excellent park, with picnic and restroom facilities, has been created around the bridge and an adjacent flour mill (1863). Walk around the area, through the covered bridge, along the banks of the Stanislaus River, and view the displays associated with the old flour mill and park's museum. Do not attempt to wade or swim in the river here. The current is deceptively swift and quite dangerous.

The oldest general store in all of California's Gold Rush Country, appropriately named "General Store," has operated continuously since 1852 in Knight's Ferry. Take time to speak with the owner, Rick Maisel, and he will share with you some of the history of his store and the town. Within the same building is the Knight's Ferry Saloon, added about 1920. Knights Ferry General Store, 17701 Main Street, P.O. Box 868, Knight's Ferry, CA 95361; 209-881-3340

The General Store.

STORE RULES 1856

1. THE STORE MUST BE OPEN FROM 6 A.M. TO 9 P.M. YEAR ROUND.

2. THE FLOOR MUST BE SWEPT, THE COUNTERS, SHELVES AND SHOWCASES MUST BE DUSTED.

3. ALL LAMPS MUST BE TRIMMED, REFILLED AND THE CHIMNEYS CLEANED; PENS MADE, DOORS AND WINDOWS OPENED, A PAIL OF WATER AND A BUCKET OF COAL MUST BE BROUGHT IN BEFORE BREAKFAST.

4. THE STORE MUST NOT BE OPENED ON SUNDAY UNLESS NECESSARY, AND THEN ONLY FOR A FEW MINUTES.

5. AN EMPLOYEE WHO IS IN THE HABIT OF SMOKING CIGARS, BEING SHAVED AT THE BARBER SHOP, GOING TO DANCES AND OTHER PLACES OF AMUSEMENT, WILL SURELY GIVE HIS EMPLOYER REASON TO BE SUSPICIOUS OF HIS HONESTY AND INTEGRITY.

6. EACH EMPLOYEE MUST GIVE NOT LESS THAN $5.00 PER YEAR TO HIS CHURCH AND MUST ATTEND CHURCH REGULARLY.

7. MEN EMPLOYEES ARE GIVEN ONE EVENING A WEEK FOR COURTING.

8. AFTER FOURTEEN HOURS OF WORK, LEISURE TIME SHOULD BE SPENT MOSTLY IN READING.

General Store Rules.

The General Store is located across from the fire station. To the east of the General Store is an old building with a sign which reads "Knight's Ferry Hotel, 1854." Whatever its past, the building is now a private residence.

After completing your tour of Knight's Ferry, drive east on CA 120 to its intersection with CA 49. Proceed south to Chinese Camp or north to Jamestown.

STANISLAUS COUNTY TRAVEL INFORMATION

CONVENTION AND VISITORS BUREAU
Telephone: 800-266-4282
Mailing and street address: 1114 J Street, Modesto, CA 95353.

Chapter Seven

TUOLUMNE COUNTY

Tuolumne County is one of the popular tourist destinations in California's Gold Rush Country. The county is home to Columbia State Historic Park, a restored Gold Rush town. The City Hotel at Columbia is widely acclaimed as the best fine dining restaurant in California's Gold Rush Country. The Groveland Hotel is distinguished as the oldest hotel in California's Gold Rush Country. With 4 historic hotels (The Groveland Hotel, The Jamestown Hotel, The Gunn House, and The City Hotel) and an abundance of modern hotels, motels, bed & breakfasts, RV facilities, and restaurants in Sonora and Jamestown, the area is a natural overnight stop. Tuolumne County, in addition to being rich in landmarks and historic sites, is rich in scenic beauty. Wildflowers grace the hills in April and May in colorful profusion.

Tuolumne County has been the setting for more than 300 movies and television shows since 1919 when Universal Pictures filmed segments from *The Red Glove* near Sonora. Movies filmed in Tuolumne County at Columbia, Sonora, and Jamestown, include *High Noon* (1952), *For Whom the Bell Tolls* (1943), *Apache* (1954), *Big Country* (1958), *Dodge City* (1939), and *The Virginian* (1924). More recently, the area has served as the setting for *Back to the Future III*, Clint Eastwood's *Unforgiven,* and *The Great American West*. While these films are a part of modern history, all are cast in periods reminiscent of the Gold Rush.

As you drive on CA 49 from Chinese Camp to Jamestown and walk the streets of Sonora and Columbia State Historic Park, you may recognize the settings for many western movies.

BIG OAK FLAT/GROVELAND

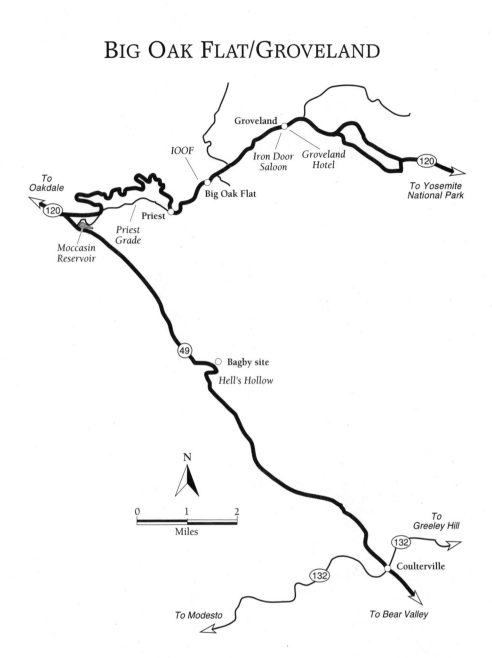

Just north of the Mariposa County-Tuolumne County border on CA 49, CA 120 branches off to the east and the mountain towns of Big Oak Flat and Groveland.

To reach Groveland from CA 49, turn east on CA 120 at Moccasin. There is a small powerhouse here, a part of the Hetch Hetchy project which provides electricity for San Francisco. About 0.5 mile from CA 49, you will have a choice of CA 120 or Old Priest's Grade Road. Old Priest's

Grade Road is essentially straight up the hill for 2 miles and is definitely the shorter of the 2 routes. Do NOT attempt to drive this road with a RV or while pulling any kind of trailer. If you follow CA 120, you will travel 4 miles to where the roads join at Priest. Continue 3 miles to Big Oak Flat. On the left you will see an imposing old building (1853) which houses the local chapter of the International Order of Odd Fellows (I.O.O.F.). Just 0.2 mile farther is another old, unidentified building that appears to be from the same era. Continue on to Groveland 4 miles ahead.

GROVELAND

As you enter Groveland from the west, you descend a slight hill which gives an overview of the hills beyond and the town below.

The Groveland Hotel (1849) has thick adobe walls and is of Monterey Colonial Architectural Style. An addition was constructed in 1914 to accommodate workers on the nearby O'Shaughnessy Dam project, one of several used to provide water and electricity for San Francisco and other towns. The Groveland Hotel, besides being the oldest, is among the best decorated of the historic hotels in California's Gold Rush Country. Each of its 17 rooms are decorated in Old World Style with soft beds and comforters and European antiques. The Groveland Hotel, 18767 Main Street, Groveland, CA 95321; 800-273-3314 or 209-962-4000; FAX 209-962-6674.

Groveland Hotel.

Water skiing is very popular on Don Pedro Lake.

The Iron Door Saloon (1850) is the oldest saloon in California's Gold Rush Country. The saloon is named for its massive iron doors which were shipped around Cape Horn from England; 209-962-8904.

After you have savored Groveland's best, if you are headed for Yosemite National Park, drive east. If you are ready to continue north on CA 49, head west up the hill on CA 120. The drive down Old Priest's Grade Road provides a great view of the valley below. Remember, no trailers, no motor coaches, and no one faint of heart.

Chinese Camp is just 6 miles beyond Moccasin and CA 120 joins CA 49 for this distance. For the first 3 miles of the drive, Don Pedro Lake is on the right. Take time to pull off to the right at 1 of several scenic overlooks to contemplate the Tuolumne River now deep below the water of this large recreation area. Don Pedro Lake offers numerous water related recreational activities.

CHINESE CAMP

Known originally as Camp Washington, the name was changed to Chinese Camp because of the large number of Chinese, estimated to be 5,000, who mined here after 1849. Chinese Camp is distinguished as the only "town settled by the Chinese" in California's Gold Rush Country, according to the Tuolumne County Historical Society.

CHINESE CAMP OVERVIEW

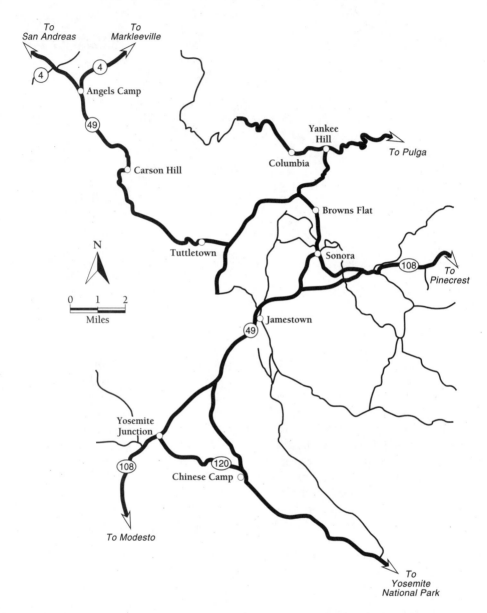

As small as Chinese Camp may appear today, there are a number of historic structures to be seen. The McAdams Store building (1854) is on Main Street about 200 feet west of CA 49. The I.O.O.F. building (1854), now a private residence, is on the southwestern corner of CA 49 and Main Street.

CHINESE CAMP

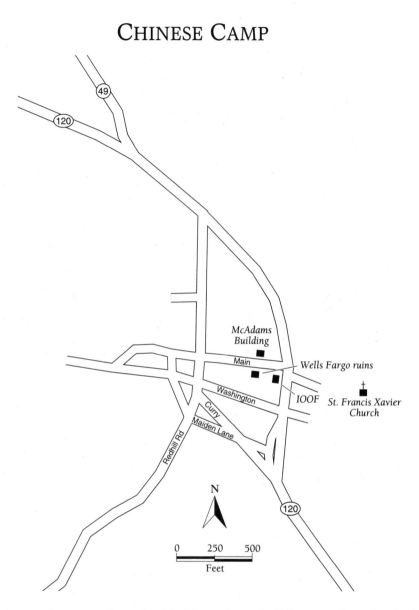

Across the street from the McAdams Store building are the ruins (a small portion of the original adobe wall) of the Wells, Fargo & Company building (1849). The picturesque St. Francis Xavier Catholic Church (1854), stands on a hill overlooking Chinese Camp on the east side of CA 49. The small cemetery behind the church has a number of interesting tombstones.

A colorful side trip from Chinese Camp in the springtime is the area known locally as the Redhills Road or the Red Hills Recreation Area. Wildflowers paint the "red hills" here with beautiful displays in April and May. Take Redhills Road from Main Street (100 yards west of the McAdams Store) and turn left or south and follow this road for 5 miles to the LaGrange Road. About 0.5 mile from central Chinese Camp, on the right, is the local school, which resembles a Chinese pagoda.

At 1 mile, turn left (Sims Road joins Redhills Road from the right) and proceed along the creek to LaGrange Road for 3 miles. Please note that there are no bridges here so some water may be flowing over the road where the road crosses the creek. The road is paved and unless the water is deep, there should be no problem in crossing. At 0.25 mile before Redhills Road intersects with LaGrange Road (County Road J59), there are remnants from the foundation of the Crimea House on the left. Behind these ruins is 1 of several old stone corrals in the area. The corrals could be built easily from the numerous stones in the fields and obviously are durable.

The area across J59 (to the west) is the site of the so-called Tong War fought in September 1856. The skirmish was between 900 Yan Woos and 1,200 Sam Yaps with 4 combatants reportedly killed. If you are planning to visit Knight's Ferry (See Stanislaus County, page 50), turn right (north) on J59 and proceed 3 miles to CA 108/CA 120. Knight's Ferry is another 9 miles from this intersection to the west. If not, return to Chinese Camp and proceed north on CA 49. If your timing is right, at 1 mile north of Chinese Camp, you might see one of the Sierra Railway steam engines from Railtown 1897 puffing across the valley with black smoke belching into the crisp blue sky.

Two miles north of Chinese Camp, CA 49 intersects with CA 108. Straight ahead is Table Mountain, a flat lava ridge, which dominates the skyline from Knight's Ferry to Columbia. The ridge was the site of a number of successful mines. The area's second old stone corral is 0.75 mile to the left on CA 108, on the right side of the road. Also to the left on CA 120/CA 108, 12 miles away, is Knight's Ferry. Jamestown is 4 miles to the right on CA 49/CA 108.

JAMESTOWN

Locals often prefer to call the town "Jimtown" after George F. James, a lawyer who settled here in 1848. Jamestown and the surrounding area is perhaps best known for its role in numerous western movies, including *Back To The Future III* and Clint Eastwoods *Unforgiven*, and the popular 1960's television show *Petticoat Junction*. The Sierra Railway Engine No. 3 was a familiar sight in the *Petticoat Junction* town of Hooterville.

The railroad's 26-acre complex is now preserved as Railtown 1897 in Jamestown. The railway's large collection of rolling stock and its roundhouse make Railtown 1897 a favorite setting for western-themed movies. The attraction is well marked with frequent signs from CA 49. Visitors can tour the Sierra Railroad shops and park daily, 9:30 A.M. to 4:30 P.M., except Thanksgiving, Christmas, and New Year's Day. Trains operate

Railtown 1897's Engine #2 on a tour near Jamestown.

JAMESTOWN

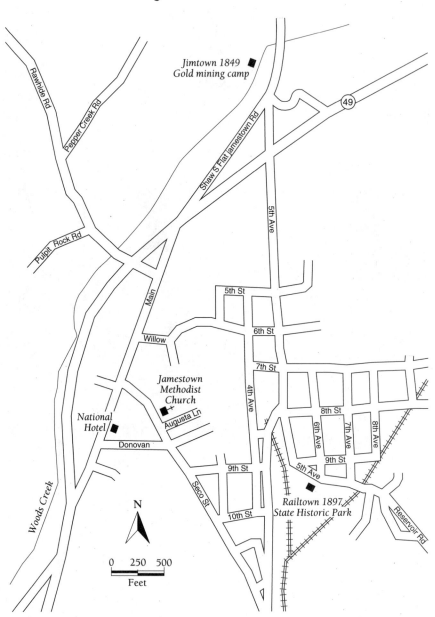

Jimtown 1849
Gold mining camp

Rawhide Rd

Pepper Creek Rd

Shaw S Flat Jamestown Rd

49

5th Ave

Pulpit Rock Rd

Main

5th St

6th St

Willow

7th St

Jamestown
Methodist
Church

4th Ave

8th St

National
Hotel

Augusta Ln

6th Ave

7th Ave

8th Ave

Donovan

9th St

Woods Creek

9th St

5th Ave

Seco St

Railtown 1897
State Historic Park

Reservoir Rd

N

10th St

0   250   500

Feet

hourly from 11 A.M. to 3 P.M., weekends, April through September and
Saturdays only, October and November. Guided tours are $2 for adults
and $1 for youths (6-12). Train rides are $6 adults and $3 for youths.
Railtown 1897, Fifth Avenue at Reservoir Road, P.O. Box 1250,
Jamestown 95327, 209-984-3953; FAX 209-984-4936.

A number of interesting places can be seen in Jamestown. Most are modern, however, and all are concentrated along Main Street which branches off CA 49 at the Chevron Service Station and runs parallel to CA 49 for 0.5 mile before rejoining the highway.

The National Hotel, which has operated continuously since 1859 at 77 Main Street, is well known for its food and wine festivals. The hotel has many original furnishings (along with the appropriate modern conveniences) which create an authentic "gold rush era" stay for guests. The bar is the original. For reservations, call 209-984-3446 or 800-894-3446 in California or 800-446-1333, Extension 286, outside of California.

The Jamestown United Methodist Church (1852), according to church records, was "Built and paid for in 1852 partly by the gamblers and partly by the good people of Jamestown for the use of all sects on Sundays and for educational purposes on week days." The Jamestown United Methodist Church is located at 18193 Seco Street. Visitors are welcome to attend Sunday services which begin at 11 A.M.

A recommended modern (yet with an air of historic authenticity) commercial gold panning operation is located in Jamestown. Set up to replicate an 1849 gold mining camp, the camp is appropriately named JIMTOWN 1849 Gold Mining Camp. JIMTOWN 1849 is located on Woods Creek at 18170 Main Street on the west side of CA 49. Amateur miners (adults and children) can experience gold panning with a good probability of finding flakes and a few small nuggets. JIMTOWN 1849 Gold Mining Camp, closed only on Christmas Day, opens at 9 A.M. and closes at 5 P.M. in the winter and "about 7 P.M." in the summer. Prices vary by the level of the experience desired. One person panning in Woods Creek will start at $10; a family of 5 begins at $20. JIMTOWN 1849 Gold Mining Camp can be discovered on the Internet at http://www.goldprospecting.com. Mail: P.O. Box 1040, Jamestown 95327; 209-984-4653; FAX 209-984-0711.

After touring Jamestown, continue north on CA 49/CA 108 Business Route a few miles to Sonora. Please note that you merge to the right 1.5 miles from central Jamestown where the CA 108 Bypass leads east and CA 49/CA 108 Business Route turns to north.

SONORA

Sonora, also known as Sonorian Camp, was founded by Mexicans. Known as the Queen of the Southern Mines, Sonora is distinguished in California's Gold Rush Country in a number of ways. Sonora's mines proved to be among the richest and Sonora is one of the more picturesque towns. The St. James Episcopal Church (1859), known as the Red Church, stands on Piety Hill in Sonora. This church is considered to be the most scenic and is perhaps the most photographed church in California's Gold Rush Country. The Bonanza Mine, also located on Piety Hill, proved to be the largest and richest pocket mine (a large quan-

The Sonora Days Inn.

tity of gold nuggets concentrated in one area) in California's Gold Rush Country.

Sonora is the setting for the first traffic light on northbound CA 49 in central Sonora at Stockton Street and South Washington Street.

The oldest building in Sonora is the historic Gunn House (1850). The Gunn House is located just 1.5 blocks from CA 49 and adjacent to the old Sonora Opera House (1885) on South Washington Street. The Gunn House's heritage is traced to Dr. Lewis C. Gunn who sailed around Cape Horn in 1849 and settled in Sonora with his family. He built a 2 story adobe structure in 1850. Gunn printed the Sonora Herald in the front parlor, the first newspaper published in California's Gold Rush Country on July 4, 1850. The Gunn House has been a hospital and private residence.

Today, after remodeling and additions, the Gunn House is furnished in comfortable period decor. Each room has all modern conveniences with the exception of telephones. The Gunn House, 286 South Washington Street, Sonora, CA 95370. For room or dining reservations, call 209-533-4111; FAX 209-533-3835.

Although built long after the Gold Rush ended, The Sonora Days Inn nevertheless has ties to the Gold Rush. The Sonora Days Inn has played an integral part in the film industries work here to create western and Gold Rush themed movies. The Sonora Days Inn dates to 1896 when it was opened as the Hotel Victoria. After a fire in 1923 destroyed much of its façade, the building was remodeled and opened as The Sonora Inn in 1931.

SONORA

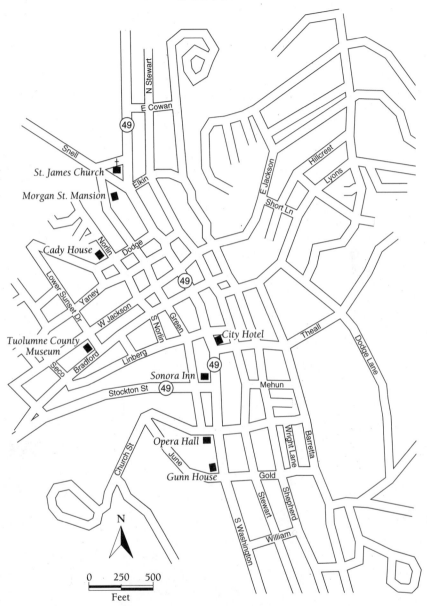

A small darkroom, where the film crews worked to develop film shot on location in the area, operated in the basement for many years. Crew members often "autographed" the walls of the room with their names, the names of their studios, and the movies they were working on. A number of these names are still visible today. Ask at the front desk for a tour of this area of the hotel.

The Sonora Days Inn, 160 South Washington Street, Sonora, CA 95370. For reservations, call 209-532-2400. Clint Eastwood reportedly favors The Sonora Days Inn when he is in town filming one of his movies. You might ask for the suite that Clint Eastwood prefers. Canterbury Restaurant serves a complete menu 24 hours daily.

The Tuolumne County Museum (1866) is housed in the former county jailhouse. Iron bars still cover some of the windows. Excellent exhibits present county history, the Gold Rush, and the Overland Trails over the Sierra Nevada. The Tuolumne County Museum is located at 158 West Bradford Avenue. The Hall, Kinney, and Baker homes, all Victorian style homes, are adjacent. The Tuolumne County Museum, P.O. Box 299, Sonora, CA 95370. (209) 532-1317. Weekdays: 10 A.M. to 4 P.M. daily. Sundays, Memorial Day through Labor Day, 10 A.M. to 4 P.M.

TOURING SONORA

The historic district of Sonora runs from the top of Piety Hill on the northern end to The Gunn House on the southern end. Most of the historic buildings are along Washington Street (the main street through central Sonora). Start at either end, or in the middle, and walk along both sides of Washington Street (North and South) to see this area. The St. James Episcopal Church (a.k.a. the "Red Church") stands at the top of Piety Hill and adjacent to the equally red Street-Morgan Mansion (1896).

Among the many highlights along North and South Washington Streets are the I.O.O.F. building (1850s), the City Hotel (1852) and the re-

Historic buildings line North Washington Street in Sonora.

cently refurbished Opera Hall (1885). You will be amazed at the grandeur of what was once the belle of the area. The ultimate in early "prefab" homes, The Cady House (72 North Norlin Street, corner of Dodge and North Norlin) was shipped around Cape Horn with numbered pieces and assembled here sometime in the 1850s.

Many activities are scheduled during the year in Sonora. The popular Mother Lode Roundup, a rodeo event held each Mother's Day Weekend in May, includes a parade with many floats, bands, and horses. The Tuolumne County Wild West Film Fest, held on the last weekend of September, is another popular event. The Mother Lode Fairgrounds on the south entrance to Sonora has an event scheduled, ranging from rodeos to flea markets, almost every weekend from March through November.

Sonora is the gateway to numerous Sierra Nevada mountain resorts and seasonal recreational areas.

After exploring Sonora, drive north on CA 49 up and over Piety Hill for 3 miles. Turn right at Parrot's Ferry Road and follow the signs for 2 miles to Columbia State Historic Park. There are no entrance gates or fees. Park in 1 of the several designated parking areas.

COLUMBIA STATE HISTORIC PARK

Known as the Gem of the Southern Mines, Columbia's role in the Gold Rush and its importance today in California's Gold Rush Country is second only to that of the Sutter's Mill Site at Marshall Gold Discovery State Historic Park in Coloma. With more than 250 acres incorporated into the Columbia State Historic Park, visitors have an excellent opportunity to vicariously experience the Gold Rush. Visitors can ride an authentic stagecoach, sleep in an old hotel, shop in replicas of Gold Rush era stores and chat with docents clad in period clothing. If not for the pavement on the streets and the parking lots surrounding Columbia State Historic Park, one could easily imagine that the Gold Rush was still happening in Columbia.

Gold was discovered at Columbia on March 27, 1850 by Dr. Thadeus Hildreth. Although first named Hildreth's Diggins for its discoverer, the town was soon named Columbia. Columbia grew to a town of more than 5,000 people with 150 saloons, shops, and stores and other businesses catering to the gold miners. Following fires which swept through Columbia in 1854 and 1857, the town was rebuilt with fireproof brick.

Columbia proved to be the richest area in California's Gold Rush Country. More than $1.5 billion in gold, at today's prices, was removed from the area around Columbia. The huge rocks which surround Columbia, almost surreal in their appearance, were exposed as miners removed topsoil to a depth of about 60 feet. Columbia was originally a "dry diggins," When water was finally brought to Columbia in 1853, sluice operations speeded up the removal of gold rich topsoil.

COLUMBIA

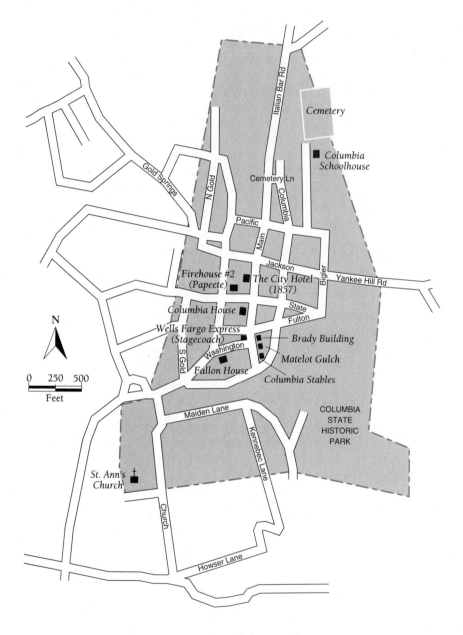

In 1945, the State of California purchased Columbia and renamed the old town as the Columbia State Historic Park. Columbia is the best preserved of all of the old mining towns in California's Gold Rush Country.

Wells, Fargo and Company Building in Columbia State Historic Park.

TOURING COLUMBIA STATE HISTORIC PARK

All of Columbia has been designated a historic district. Every building is either an original or, in a few cases, a recreation. All have been refurbished or restored. Central Columbia is essentially 2 blocks wide and 3 blocks long. Its current size is a small portion of its size at the height of the Gold Rush. All operating businesses are manned by docents or business owners dressed in period costume to recreate an 1850-1870 Gold Rush town.

A good point to begin your tour of Columbia is at the intersection of Fulton and Main Street, in front of the Wells, Fargo Stage Stop.

The Wells, Fargo & Company building (1858) is the dominant building in Columbia State Historic Park. More than 1.4 million ounces of gold were weighed in on the scales on display at the Wells, Fargo & Company office here. Wells, Fargo & Company stagecoaches regularly departed from Columbia carrying gold and passengers bound for San Francisco, Mariposa and Placerville.

A favorite of visitors, an authentic stagecoach operates through the streets and the nearby "canyon area" of the "diggins." Buy your tickets at the Wells Fargo Stage Stop for rides on the stagecoach. If the weather is good, go for one of the "shotgun" seats beside the driver. The view is best from there. Stagecoach rides usually last 15 minutes.

Located north of the Wells Fargo Stage Stop, the Columbia Riding Stable offers a variety of rides on horses and ponies for the beginning rider to the most experienced rider. Rides can take as little as 0.5 hour

Matelot Gulch is a popular place for gold panning.

A favorite stop in Columbia is the Candy Kitchen.

for a guided tour around Columbia's streets (just line up for these rides) or as long as 1 day (by advance reservation only). Check with the agents for fares for the stagecoach, horse and pony rides. Columbia Stage Line and Stable, P.O. Box 1777, Columbia 95310; 209-532-0663, 209-736-0225; e-mail, intreped@goldrush.com.

Matelot Gulch Mine Store is on Main Street between the Columbia Riding Stable and the Wells Fargo Stage Stop. Surrounded by huge boulders washed clean by the 49ers, adults and children can pan for gold. Purchase a bucket of dirt and try your luck here. Nothing is guaranteed but fun for everyone is almost certain. Matelot Gulch Mine Store, P.O. Box 28, Columbia, CA 95310; 209-532-9693.

From Matelot Gulch, proceed straight ahead down Fulton Street, beside the big freight wagon, past the Columbia Gazette Building (1855) to the Fallon Hotel and Theatre (1859). The Fallon Hotel Theatre serves as the stage for the Columbia Actors' Repertory. CAR offers 8 major productions during the annual 12-month season.

In front of the Fallon Hotel is the Masonic Hall (1949). This building is a reconstruction to replace an earlier 3-story building built in 1854 and is an excellent example of restoration at Columbia State Historic Park.

Return to the front of the Wells, Fargo & Co. Building and walk north on Main Street. On your left is the El Capitan National Bank, a real bank in a historic setting. On your right, at the corner of State Street and Main Street is The Brady Building.

Other Main Street favorites include the Douglas Saloon (1857), a great place for a sarsaparilla; the Candy Kitchen, my favorite for old fashioned candies—watch it being twisted in the window; the Columbia House (1850), an excellent place for family dining; and Towpe & Leavitt, the place to buy souvenirs. At the far end of town, on the corner of Main Street and Jackson, the Columbia Mercantile offers groceries, film and sundries in an old fashioned store.

Small museums are set up along Main Street and include the Justice Court and Rebecca's Hall. The Columbia Museum, at the corner of State Street and Main, houses an excellent collection of Gold Rush memorabilia.

The City Hotel, near the north end of Columbia on Main Street, was first built in 1856 and was known then as the What Cheer House. A fire destroyed the structure in 1867. Rebuilt in 1871, the hotel has been known as The City Hotel since 1874. For guests with rooms along Main Street, a balcony provides an excellent view of downtown.

The City Hotel Dining Room is noted throughout California's Gold Rush Country for first class service and its fine cuisine prepared and served by students from Columbia College with assistance from professional staff. In coordination with its sister hotel, the Fallon Hotel, guests are offered weekend stays with dinner at the City Hotel Dining Room and theater at the Fallon Hotel Theatre. Contact The City Hotel, P.O. Box 1870, Columbia, CA 95310; 209-532-1479.

Mark Twain's cabin at Jackass Hill.

TUOLUMNE COUNTY TRAVEL INFORMATION

TUOLUMNE COUNTY VISITORS BUREAU
Telephone (800) 446-1333; FAX (209) 533-0956
Mailing Address: P.O. Box 4020, Sonora, CA 95370
Street Address: 55 West Stockton Street
E-mail: http//www.lode.com@nsierra/visitor/

Chapter Eight

CALAVERAS COUNTY

Calaveras County is known throughout the world, perhaps better than any of the other counties in California's Gold Rush Country, because of the writings of Samuel Clemens. Clemens, who used the pen name of Mark Twain, wrote his famous story, "The Celebrated Jumping Frog of Calaveras County," after visits to Angels Camp. Black Bart, the best known of the Gold Rush bandits, began and ended his career in Calaveras County. The largest gold nugget discovered in California's Gold Rush Country was found at Carson Hill.

Residents often describe Calaveras County as a number of quiet towns with lots of country in between. Visitors are likely to agree. Motorists will be especially pleased to learn that there is not a single traffic signal in all of Calaveras County. During April and May, Calaveras County's hills are colored with spring wildflowers.

Driving north on CA 49, to reach Calaveras County, visitors cross the New Melones Bridge at the site of Robinson's Ferry (1848) which crossed the Stanislaus River, now deep below the waters of this popular water recreation area. Stop at the overlook 0.5 mile above the lake for an expansive view of the area. One mile beyond is Carson Hill.

The largest gold nugget in California's Gold Rush Country was found in 1854 at Carson Hill. The nugget weighed in at 195 pounds. Mining operations continue at Carson Hill today. The mine is closed to the public.

One mile beyond Carson Hill, literally one hundred feet away from CA 49, is the Romaggi House (1856). Its continued survival, despite its lack of preservation or maintenance, is a tribute to its sturdy construction.

CALAVERAS COUNTY

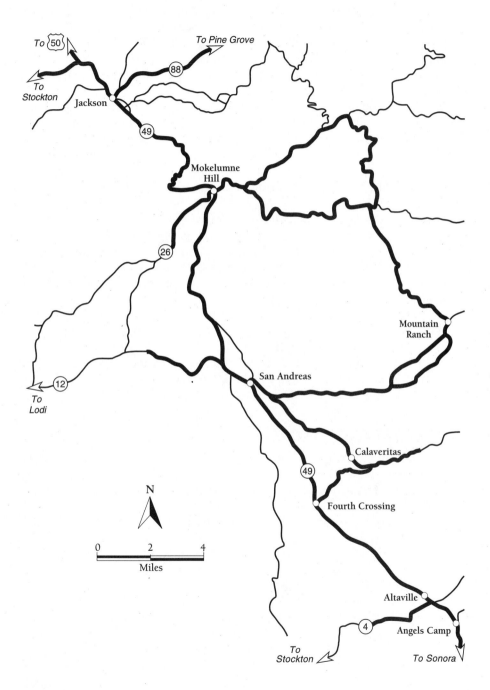

To 50

To Pine Grove

To Stockton

88

Jackson

49

Mokelumne Hill

26

Mountain Ranch

12

To Lodi

San Andreas

Calaveritas

N

49

0 2 4
Miles

Fourth Crossing

Altaville

4

Angels Camp

To Stockton

To Sonora

ANGELS CAMP

Angels Camp was named for Henry Angel, the town's first store-keeper. The Utica Mine was the most famous of the area's gold mines, producing gold until 1942. There were more than 200 stamp mills operating around the clock at Angels Camp during the period 1880 and 1890. Local legend says that when they ceased operating, the town was so quiet that people had trouble sleeping.

Even though Mark Twain was an accomplished writer, it was his short story, "The Celebrated Jumping Frog of Calaveras County," first published in the *New York Saturday Press*, that brought him fame. The first Jumping Frog Jubilee was held in 1928 to celebrate the paving of Main Street in Angels Camp in a style commemorative of its Gold Rush heritage. The winner was "Pride of San Joaquin" with a jump of 3 feet and 6 inches.

Calaveras County has since celebrated Mark Twain's famous story with yearly events now held at the Calaveras County Fairgrounds at Frogtown, two miles south of Angels Camp. Tom Sawyer and Becky Thatcher of Hannibal, Missouri, are yearly visitors to The Jumping Frog Jubilee, which attracts locals and tourists to its carnival atmosphere highlighted by frog jumping contests.

On the stage of The Jumping Frog Jubilee, frogs are dropped on the "launch" pad and encouraged by their owners to make 3 jumps. The record jump is 21 feet, 5.75 inches.

The Frog Jumping Jubilee is held the 3rd weekend of May. For information, contact the Jumping Frog Jubilee, P.O. Box 489, Angels Camp, CA 95222; 209-736-2561; FAX 209-736-2476.

TOURING ANGELS CAMP

The town of Angels Camp's buildings look similar to the way they did during the Gold Rush. Even though most of the earliest buildings have burned, Angels Camp has rebuilt in a style reminiscent of the Gold Rush.

Start your tour at the Calaveras Lodging & Visitors Association at 1301 South Main Street, at the intersection of CA 49, Bird Way, and CA 4. The Visitors Association is on the east side of CA 49 at the southern entrance to Angels Camp. Directly across the street is a statue to the "jumping frog" which has brought enduring fame to Angels Camp and Calaveras County.

Across Bird Way is the former Angels Hotel (1855). The building is now an auto parts store. Mark Twain, who lived at nearby Jackass Hill in Tuolumne County (See page 72) in 1864 and 1865, visited Angels Camp. The Angels Hotel is where Ross Coon, the proprietor, told Mark Twain the story that Twain later embellished and wrote as "The Celebrated Jumping Frog of Calaveras County."

ANGELS CAMP

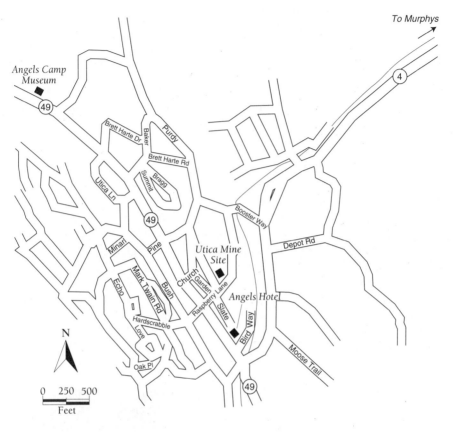

To Murphys

Angels Camp
Museum

Brett Harte Dr
Purdy
Baker
Brett Harte Rd
Utica Ln
Summit
Bragg
Booster Way
Depot Rd
Minarl
Pine
Utica Mine
Site
Echo
Mark Twain Rd
Bush
Church
Garden
Raspberry Lane
Slate
Angels Hotel
Bird Way
Hardscrabble
Love
Moose Trail
Oak Pl

N

0   250   500
Feet

Bird Way, along Angels Creek, was the site of Chinatown and the Red Light District.

A walk along Main Street will take you past notable reminders of the early Gold Rush days. They include the Love House (c. 1850), the oldest remaining building in Angels Camp, the Peirano Building (c.1854), the E. & G. Stickle Building (1856), and the I.O.O.F. building (1860). The Masonic Hall (c.1850) is on Bush Street.

Angels Camp is colorful in the fall. Foliage reflects gold in Angels Creek which crosses under CA 49 at the junction of Bird Way, CA 4, and CA 49.

The Angels Camp Museum, 0.75 mile north of central Angels Camp, houses interesting artifacts from the Gold Rush. Angels Camp Museum, 753 South Main Street, Angels Camp, CA 95222; 209-736-2963.

Altaville, 2 miles north of central Angels Camp, was founded in 1852. Altaville is best remembered as the site of an apparent hoax involving the so-called Calaveras Skull. The skull was reportedly "discovered" in the Mattison Mine in 1866 and authenticated as belonging to a prehistoric man by the state geologist. Modern dating techniques place the skull in not so prehistoric times. Even Bret Harte challenged its status as prehistoric in his poem, "To the Pliocene Skull."

There are 2 well preserved buildings at Altaville from the Gold Rush that are near CA 49. The Altaville Grammar School (1858) stands in a shady grove of trees in a small park on the west side of CA 49. The school was constructed with funds raised from a dance held at the nearby Prince-Garibardi Building (1857). The building is on the west side of CA 49, near Demerest Street, and houses a business.

MURPHYS

One of the most, if not the most, popular towns in California's Gold Rush Country is Murphys. To reach Murphys from Angels Camp, drive 9 miles east on CA 4 or from the north side of Angels Camp, take Murphys Grade Road. If you choose CA 4, you will pass Vallecito at 4 miles. Turn right on Angels Street for 0.25 mile to Main Street. On the right is the Dinkelspiel Store (1851) which is no longer open to the public. Turn left on Main Street and rejoin CA 4 about 0.75 mile.

Three miles farther on CA 4, you will reach Douglas Flat, which is located on the Central Hill Channel, an ancient river deposit rich in gold. There are several old buildings of interest on Main Street, on the north side of CA 4. They are the Gilleado (or Gileardo) Building (1851) and the

Angels Camp Museum.

Douglas Flat School House (1854). Scars on the hillside behind the school house are indications of the extensive hydraulic mining activity that took place here.

A few miles ahead, turn left from CA 4 and enter Main Street at Murphys.

Murphys, known as the "Queen of the Sierra," is one of the few Gold Rush towns of any size not in California's Highway 49. Possibly because of this, Murphys has retained much of its original charm and many of its historic buildings.

Most of its earliest buildings were lost in a fire that swept the town in 1859. Murphys (also known as Murphys Flat and Murphys Diggins) was named after brothers Daniel and John Murphy who arrived here in 1848. They set up a trading post and first mined along Angels Creek, which runs through the town.

The dominant building in Murphys, the Murphys Historic Hotel & Lodge (1861), was first built in 1856 as the Sperry and Perry's Hotel. The building burned, along with most of the others in town, in 1859 and was rebuilt in 1861. The Murphys Historic Hotel & Lodge looks like a true Gold Rush hotel, perhaps explaining its popularity.

Famous guests here have included Mark Twain, Horatio Algier, U. S. Grant, and C. E. Bolton (alias Black Bart, the stagecoach robber whose career ended in the Calaveras County Courthouse in nearby San Andreas). The Murphys Historic Hotel was once the overnight stopping point for those who traveled on the Matteson Stage on their way to the

Murphys Hotel.

Murphys Overview

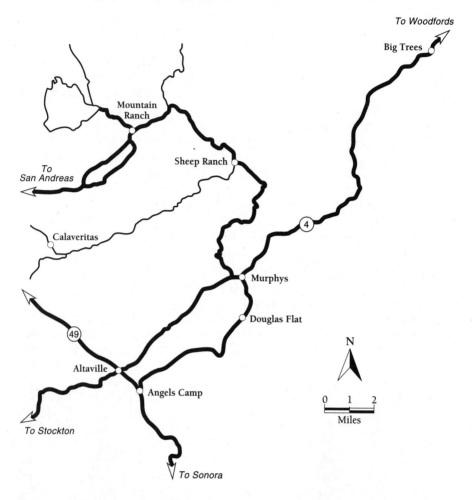

To Woodfords

Big Trees

Mountain Ranch

Sheep Ranch

To San Andreas

Calaveritas

4

Murphys

Douglas Flat

N

49

Altaville

Angels Camp

0 1 2
Miles

To Stockton

To Sonora

Calaveras Big Trees (now known as the Calaveras Big Trees State Park). Still a popular destination, this park is fifteen miles north of Murphys, near Arnold, on CA 4. Murphys Historic Hotel & Lodge, 457 Main Street, P.O. Box 329, Murphys 95247. 800-532-7684 or 209-728-3444.

TOURING MURPHYS

Like most towns in California's Gold Rush Country, Murphys's Main Street is the center of attraction. A walk along Main Street in Murphys will allow you to see most of the historic buildings. A good starting point is the Murphys Historic Hotel & Lodge at the intersection of Main Street and Algiers Street. Walk east along Main Street to Jones Street and back on the north side to Church Street, then turn right and walk east on

Church Street. On either side of Main Street and Church Street you will find a number of homes and business buildings that date to the 1850s and 1860s. The total distance is under a mile.

Notable among these are the Dunbar/Fisk Saloon (1859) at 425 Main Street, the Vassaelo/Ruiseco & Orengo/Segale Store (1859) at 419 Main Street and the Heinsdorff/Thorpe Bakery Building (1851) at 494 Main Street, whose 2-foot-thick walls have helped the building to survive numerous fires which have swept through Murphys. The Bonnet/Compere Store (1858), one of the prettiest stone structures in California's Gold Rush Country, was built of rhyolite blocks and limestone rubble and stands at 570 Main, corner of Church Street. The Chase House, at 350 Main Street, is where Albert A. Michelson, the first American scientist to be awarded the Nobel Prize, lived as a child.

The Peter L. Traver Building (1856) at 470 Main Street, was one of a few buildings to survive the 1859 fire. The building houses the Old-Timers Museum which features period and area artifacts. Hours are 11 A.M. to 4 P.M., Friday to Sunday. 209-728-1160.

Adjacent to the Old-Timers Museum is the Thompson Building (1862) at 472 Main Street. Plaques line its northern exterior wall, called the Wall of Comparative Ovations of E Clampus Vitus. Among the plaques is a sketch of Joseph Zumwalt, who founded ECV in 1850, and a drawing that depicts the often tenuous relationship between gold miners and their donkeys. The E Clampus Vitus operated during the Gold Rush as a fraternal organization whose stated purpose was to help widows and orphans. The fun-loving group often poked fun at the more organized fraternal organizations and their formal clothing. The E Clampus Vitus was reorganized in 1931 and today performs social functions as well as place plaques recognizing historic properties. They call their meeting place a "Hall of Comparative Ovations."

Joseph Zumwalt.

A number of comfortable Bed and Breakfasts have been established in historic houses at Murphys. The Dunbar House (1880) was built by Willis Dunbar, Superintendent of the Union Water Company, a forerunner of the Pacific Gas & Electric Company. The lovely Italianate style architecture building, is one of the prettiest in California's Gold Rush Country. Each bathroom comes with a claw foot bathtub. Dunbar House, 1880 Bed and Breakfast Inn, 271 Jones Street, P.O. Box 1375, Murphys, CA 95247; 800-692-6006 or 209-728-2897; FAX 209-728-1451.

The Dunbar House provides a cozy setting for a romantic weekend in Murphys.

Calaveras County and Murphys are home to a number of excellent wineries with roots to the Gold Rush. Miners from France, Germany, and Italy came to California for gold but also brought their love for wine common to their European heritage. Local wineries include the Black Sheep Winery, housed in an 1860s barn (634 French Gulch Road, at the west end of Main Street; 209-728-2157 or visit them on the internet at http://www.blacksheepwinery.com).

The Stevenot Winery, on the site of the Shaw Ranch (1860's) and 1 of the largest wineries in the Sierra Nevada, traces its roots to Gabriel Stevenot who came from Alsace (a noted wine region in eastern France along the Rhine River) in 1849. Stevenot Winery is located 2 miles northeast of Murphys, off Sheep Ranch Road at 2690 San Domingo Road; P.O. Box 345, Murphys, CA 95247; 209-728-3436; FAX: 209-728-3710.

The Kautz Ironstone Vineyards, on the site of Hay Station, an old Wells, Fargo & Company Station, is located 1 mile south of the Murphys Historic Hotel & Lodge. The winery is located at 1894 Six Mile Road, Murphys, CA 95247; 209-728-1251; FAX 209-728-1275.

When you have completed your visit to Murphys, return to Angels Camp via CA 4 or Murphys Grade Road or consider the following 2 local attractions if time permits.

MURPHYS

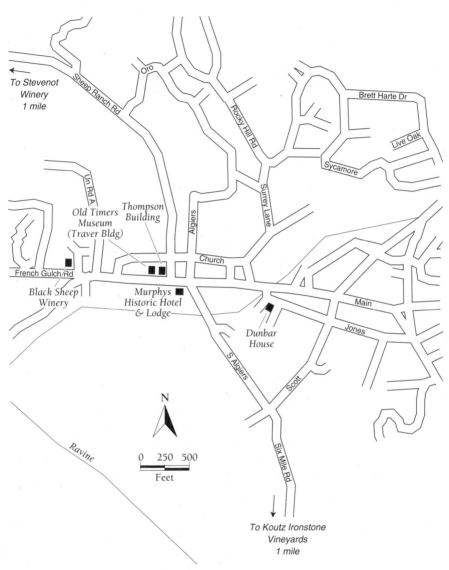

To Stevenot Winery 1 mile

Sheep Ranch Rd

Oro

Rocky Hill Rd

Brett Harte Dr

Live Oak

Sycamore

Surrey Lane

Un Rd A

Old Timers Museum (Traver Bldg)

Thompson Building

Algiers

Church

French Gulch Rd

Black Sheep Winery

Murphys Historic Hotel & Lodge

Dunbar House

Main

Jones

N

S Algiers

Scott

Ravine

0   250   500
Feet

Six Mile Rd

To Koutz Ironstone Vineyards 1 mile

CALAVERAS BIG TREES STATE PARK

Located 15 miles north of Murphys on CA 4, 2 miles beyond Arnold, a popular resort destination, the Calaveras Big Trees State Park preserves 150 giant sequoias (*Seqoiadendron giganteum*). They were discovered in the early 1850s by A. T. Dowd. After he reported his discovery, American and European newspaper and magazine writers embellished the accounts creating a "rush" to see "the big trees of Calaveras County."

Two of the giant sequoias were cut for exhibitions. In 1855, the largest tree in the forest, the "Mother of the Forest," was placed on display at the Crystal Palace in New York City for 2 years.

Visitors can easily hike among the big trees of the North Grove. The "Big Stump," where dances were held in the 1870s, is only a few yards from the parking area. The South Grove, more remote and wild, is reached by a mile-long trail. Camping is available near the North Grove. Calaveras Big Trees State Park, P.O. Box 120, Arnold, CA 95223 209-795-2334.

SHEEP RANCH

For those with the time, and the desire, to say that they have traveled all of California's Gold Rush Country, Sheep Ranch can be reached via the Sheep Ranch Road which leads from central Murphys beside the Old-Timers Museum. The road is crooked, but scenic, and drive time is about 1 hour each way to cover the 35 miles. Sheep Ranch, where the sheep roam free, is distinguished as home to the Sheep Ranch Mine, which was owned by Senator George Hearst, father of William Randolph Hearst. The young Hearst headed up Hearst Newspapers. The dominant feature at Sheep Ranch is the Pioneer Hotel, at the end of Main Street. The large building, constructed as a 1-story hotel in nearby Cheechee Flats in the 1870s, was moved to Sheep Ranch in 1904. The second story was added at that time. Return to CA 49.

The drive on CA 49 from Angels Camp to San Andreas is 11 miles. If time permits, you can take a different route off CA 49, for an additional 5 miles of back roads and beautiful countryside, to Calaveritas and the Costa Store (1852). Turn right on Fricot City Road, 3 miles north of Angels Camp, at Fourth Crossing (the stone bridge on the west of CA 49 was built in 1857 and is the 4th river crossing north of Angels Camp) about 100 yards north of the bridge. Follow this road for 3 miles to Calaveritas Road and turn left. The Costa Store is on your left in a sharp bend in the road. Continue straight ahead under the railroad crossing for 6 miles to rejoin CA 49 at San Andreas.

SAN ANDREAS

San Andreas was founded by Mexican miners in 1848. The Mexican bandit, Joaquin Murieta, was reported to operate in the area, and Black Bart was brought to trial in the courthouse here.

Murieta, most famous of the Mexican bandits, reportedly went on a 2 month crime spree in revenge for the lynching of his brother and atrocities against his girl. He is credited with killing as many as 29 people, mostly unarmed Chinese miners. Although Murieta was reportedly gunned down by a bounty hunter, many believe that Murieta returned to Mexico to live a long and peaceful life.

The Pioneer Hotel.

The feats of Black Bart are much more certain. The famous stage-coach robber, alias Black Bart (a.k.a. Charles Boles and Charles E. Bolton), had a strong dislike for Wells, Fargo & Company. He reportedly committed twenty eight robberies of stagecoaches from 1877 to 1883. Most involved Wells, Fargo & Company stagecoaches. Black Bart always walked to the site of his robbery and worked alone.

In his last robbery, near San Andreas, he dropped a handkerchief. A laundry mark on the handkerchief led to Black Bart being identified as Charles E. Bolton, a well respected resident of San Francisco. Black Bart was convicted of only one robbery, the last one, and sentenced to serve four years in the San Quentin Prison, in the San Francisco harbor. After his release, he was not heard of again.

San Andreas's historic district is located on North Main Street, where its remaining buildings are clustered together on the south side.

TOURING SAN ANDREAS

To see the highlights of San Andreas's historic district, begin at CA 49 and walk east, downhill, on North Main Street. Highlights include Gooney's Saloon Building (1858), which has served as a saloon or restaurant since its construction, and the I.O.O.F. Building (1856). The Hall of Records (1893) at 30 North Main Street is now the Calaveras County Museum and Visitors Center. It is open 10 A.M. to 4 P.M., daily, except major holidays. (209) 754-6513).

San Andreas

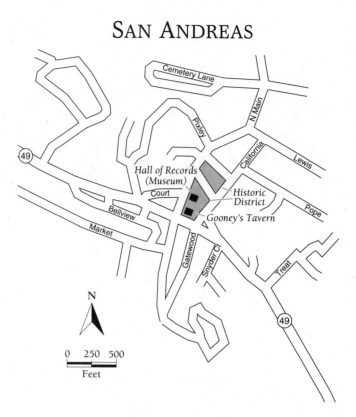

The Calaveras County Courthouse (1867), located behind the Hall of Records, was the setting for the trial of Black Bart. Visitors can see the jail cell where he was kept pending his trial. Mountain Ranch and California Caverns, where 49ers carved their names on the walls, at Cave City are excellent side trip destinations. Take Mountain Ranch Road east from central San Andreas and follow the signs for 10 miles to Mountain Ranch.

MOUNTAIN RANCH

Two old buildings here are of interest. The Dughi Building (late 1860s) is on Washington Street, off Mountain Ranch Road, at the intersection of Blacksmith Avenue. The Domenghini Building (1856), a former saloon, is just off Mountain Ranch Road on Garabaldi Street. After viewing these buildings, return to Mountain Ranch Road and drive 0.5 mile west (back toward San Andreas) and turn left on Michel Road. At 0.5 mile, turn left on Cave City Road for 1.5 miles down the hill to California Caverns. There are ample road signs here to direct you to California Caverns.

MOUNTAIN RANCH

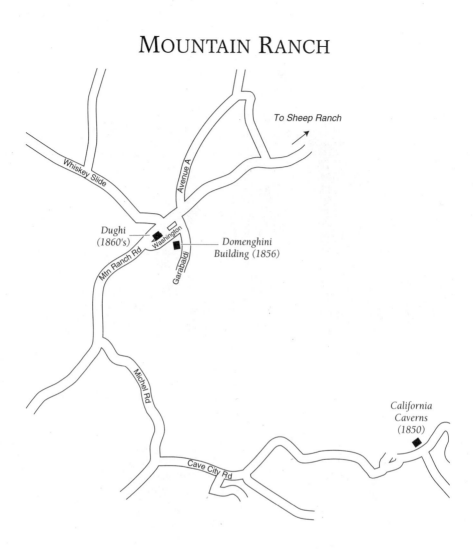

CALIFORNIA CAVERNS

The California Caverns, originally known as the Cave City Cave, were discovered in 1850. Visitors can explore, with minimal difficulty, the underground caverns where 49ers left behind their names and dates of visit in the soft limestone rock walls. B. K. Thorn, credited with the capture of Black Bart, carved his name on the wall. John Muir visited the Cave City Cave and wrote of his experiences there in *Mountains of California*. Bret Harte and Mark Twain are reported to have visited Cave City.

The "Trail of Lights" Tour is about 80 minutes long and suited for the family. The "Wild Cave" Expedition Tours are available to those who seek underground adventure. California Caverns, 9600 Cave City Road, Mountain Ranch, CA 95246; P.O. Box 78, Vallecito, CA 95251; 209-736-

California Caverns.

2708. Hours: 10 A.M. to 5 P.M., summer, 10 A.M. to 4 P.M., fall; daily, mid-May to October; weekends in winter (as long as the caverns are not flooded).

When you have completed your tour of California Caverns, return to San Andreas and CA 49. Mokelumne Hill is 8 miles north of San Andreas. At 6 miles north of San Andreas, on a long flat stretch of road, there is a marker for Chili Gulch, which was populated by a large group of Chileans.

MOKELUMNE HILL

Mokelumne Hill, one of the most important towns of the Southern Mines, had a population estimated at 15,000 during the Gold Rush. Mokelumne Hill was reputed to be the wildest town in California's Gold Rush Country. Mokelumne Hill, pronounced Mah-kell-uhm-e, is derived from a Miwuk Indian word which means "people of the village of Mukul."

The dominant landmark in Mokelumne Hill is the Hotel Léger (1854) just 0.3 mile east of CA 49 on Main Street. The Hotel Léger has been recently redecorated with period wall coverings and furniture. Guests are invited to climb out their room window (literally, as there is no door) onto the balcony for an excellent view of the surrounding town and hills. The balcony is a great place to watch the sunset or drink your morning cup of coffee.

CALAVERAS

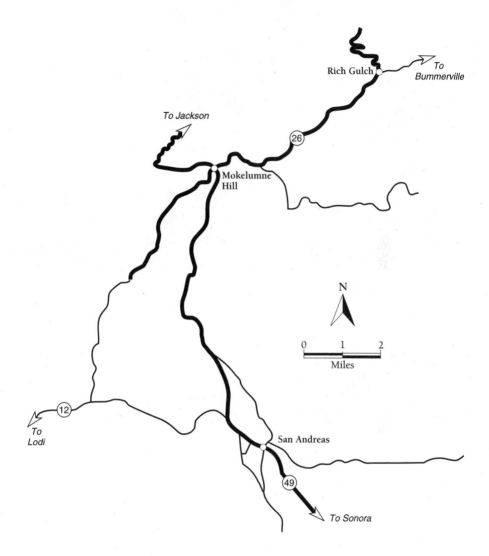

Owner Mark Jennings, a native of the area and brimming with answers to questions, specializes in ribs (recommended) and does much of the cooking for Nonno's Restaurant. The bar is authentic to the original hotel. The former Calaveras County Court House was incorporated into the Hotel Léger in 1866 after the county seat was relocated to San Andreas. The old courtroom has been turned into a banquet room. Hotel Léger, 8304 Main Street, Mokelumne Hill 95245; 209-286-1401; FAX 209-286-2105.

From the balcony of the Hotel Léger, guests enjoy a panoramic view, which includes the 3-story IOOF Building (left rear).

TOURING MOKELUMNE HILL

Central Mokelumne Hill consists of a number of historic buildings, a few turned into modern shops along Main Street and Center Street. Start your tour at the Hotel Léger by walking west, toward CA 49, on Main Street. On the right is the Congregational Church (1856), the oldest Congregational Church building in California.

Turn around and walk past the Hotel Léger and down the hill, several hundred yards, to the intersection of Main Street and Center Street. The 3-story I.O.O.F. Building (1854) first served as the Wells, Fargo & Company building with just 2 floors. The 3rd floor was added in 1861 for use by the lodge. On either side of the I.O.O.F. building are several historic buildings, most in ruins. Only the front façade of the L. Mayer & Son Building (1854) is visible.

Mokelumne Hill had a large foreign population, as evidenced by the names of various features in the area. French Hill, the site of the so-called "French War" of 1851, is the tallest hill in town. It was there that French and Americans fought over their "diggins." China Gulch Street reminds visitors of the several thousand Chinese who mined at Mokelumne Hill. Chili Gulch is 2 miles south of town.

MOKELUMNE HILL

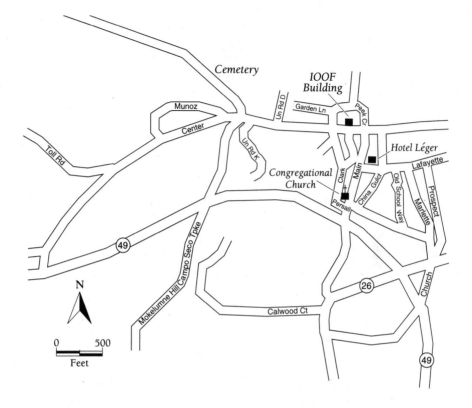

As you leave Mokelumne Hill and drive north on CA 49, you will enter a series of sharp curves and descend about 1,000 feet to the Mokelumne River and cross over to Amador County.

CALAVERAS COUNTY TRAVEL INFORMATION

CALAVERAS LODGING & VISITORS ASSOCIATION
Telephone: 800-225-3764 or 209-736-0049
Mailing Address: P.O. Box 637, Angels Camp, CA 95222
Street Address: 1211 South Main Street

Chapter Nine

AMADOR COUNTY

Amador County is rich in history and scenic drives. Like Calaveras County, there are few towns and a lot of country in between. Amador County's green hills, covered with spring wildflowers, are a favorite for back roads tours through the wine area of the Shenandoah Valley, Volcano, Daffodil Hill and Fiddletown. Fall foliage colors these same vistas each October.

As you enter Amador County on CA 49, Gardella's Inn (early 1850s) on the right side of the bridge, is the lone reminder of a number of inns constructed at the site of Big Bar. One mile farther is the Ginocchio Store (early 1850s) which sits less than 25 feet from CA 49. The Ginocchio Store, only a shell and perilously close to collapse, is the only reminder from Butte City which once had 10,000 citizens. Proceed 2 miles ahead to Jackson. As you enter Jackson, you will pass a modern shopping area on the west side of CA 49.

JACKSON

Jackson, the county seat for Amador County, was first called *Botellas*—Spanish for "bottles"—because of an abundance of bottles apparently discarded there by early travelers. Jackson reflects much of its ethnic diversity in the buildings constructed by miners and emigrants from the United States, Mexico, Serbia and Italy. The National Hotel (1862) and I.O.O.F. Building (1862) dominate the south end of Main Street. Jackson retains much of the flavor of a Gold Rush town.

AMADOR

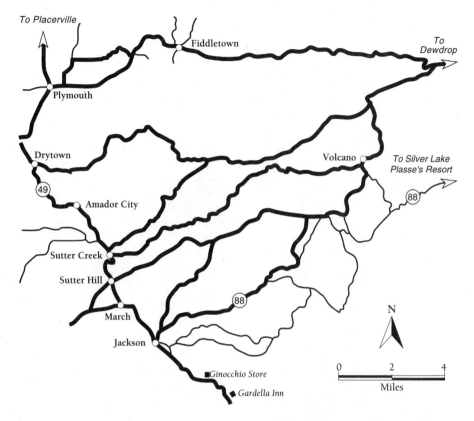

The National Hotel (1862), across the street from the I.O.O.F. Building (1862), dominates the south end of Main Street. The hotel's bar, on the first level (up the steps), is lively with entertainment most weekends. Michael's Restaurant, in the basement, serves up excellent dishes nightly. The National Hotel, 2 Water Street, Jackson, CA 95642. For rooms, call 209-223-0500. For dinner reservations, call Michael's Restaurant at 209-223-3448.

Café MAX Swiss Bakery is operated by Swiss immigrant Max and wife Lynda Eggimann who have restored this 1865 bakery and oven (originally built outside the building prior to 1865 to protect the building from burning) to its original appearance. Guests are invited to enter the kitchen to watch the oven being loaded or unload with as many as 100 loaves of the bakery's famous oven bread. Try the pasty, one of the house specialties. This hearty meat and vegetable meal, baked in a pie crust, was favored by the Cornish miners who worked in the nearby Argonaut and Kennedy Mines. Café MAX Swiss Bakery, 140 Main Street, Jackson, CA 95642; 209-223-0174; daily, 6 A.M. to 6 P.M., Sundays, 8 A.M. to 4 P.M.

Ginocchio Store (or Butte Store) stands beside Highway 49 south of Jackson.

JACKSON OVERVIEW

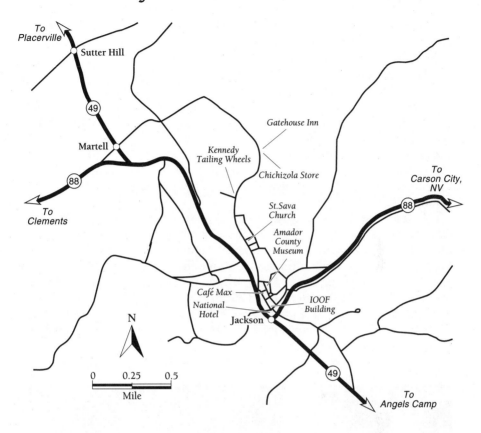

To Placerville

Sutter Hill

Martell

To Clements

Gatehouse Inn

Kennedy Tailing Wheels

Chichizola Store

St. Sava Church

Amador County Museum

Café Max

National Hotel

Jackson

IOOF Building

To Carson City, NV

N

0   0.25   0.5
Mile

To Angels Camp

The Armstead C. Brown House (1859) houses the Amador County Museum. Excellent displays of period artifacts and working models of the Argonaut and Kennedy Mines are found here. This museum is on one of the hills overlooking downtown Jackson. Excellent displays are found in the backyard and views from the back yard are great. The Amador County Museum, 225 Church Street, Jackson, CA 95642. Hours: Wednesday through Sunday, 10 A.M. to 4 P.M.; 209-223-6386.

TOURING JACKSON

A fire burned much of Jackson in August 1862. A few older buildings remain in the downtown area along Water and Main Streets. These include the Masonic Building (1854) and the Wells, Fargo Building (1857) on Water Street and the I.O.O.F. Building, reportedly the tallest 3 story building in the United States, on Main Street. On the corner of Court Street and Church Street is the magnificent St. Patrick's Catholic Church

(1868). A monument in front of the church honors Angelo Noce, a Jackson native who founded the Columbus Day Holiday.

Beyond downtown about 1 mile is the Serbian Orthodox Church of St. Sava (1894) on Jackson Gate Road. The mother church of the denomination for North America is one of the most scenic churches in California's Gold Rush Country.

The Chichizola Store (1850) [pronounced CHEEK-e-zola] was built by Agostino Chichizola at Jackson Gate, a rocky cut or "gate" through which Jackson Creek still flows. The store served miners who came here when gold was discovered in 1849. Agostino and brother Louis, with their 10-year old brother Antonio, reportedly left their native Italy in 1848 for Boston to avoid the draft. Agostino and Antonio traveled on to California via the Isthmus of Panama and San Francisco. Operating from the Chichizola Store, Agostino provided mining supplies to the adjacent Argonaut and Kennedy Mines.

Antonio moved to Indian Gulch near Hornitos (See Mariposa County, pages 38-40) where he opened a store in 1858. After success there, he moved to San Francisco and became the first president of the Bank of Italy. This bank ultimately became the Bank of America.

Visitors to the Chichizola Store can see the original safe and other reminders of its rich history. The Chichizola Store, 1324 Jackson Gate Road, Jackson, CA 95642. Mailing address: P.O. Box 1048, Sutter Creek, CA 95685; 209-223-3101; FAX 209-267-1860. Hours: Friday through Monday, 10 A.M. to 4 P.M.

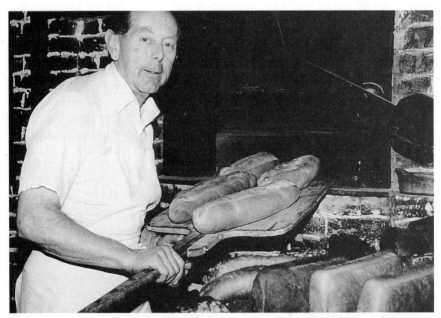

Max Eggiman takes fresh bread from his 1865 oven at Café MAX Swiss Bakery.

JACKSON—LOWER

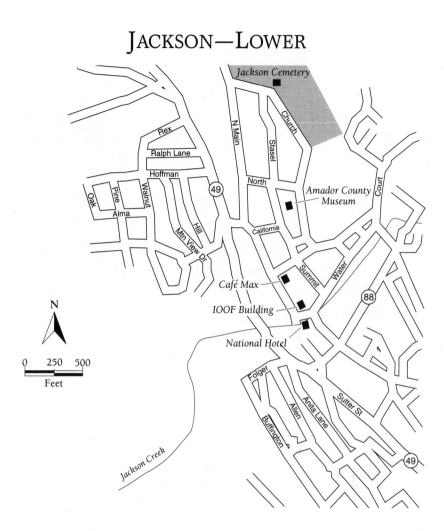

The Gate House Inn, home to 4 generations of the Chichizola family who operated the adjacent Chichizola Store (1850), is listed on the National Register of Historic Places. The Gate House, 1330 Jackson Gate Road, Jackson, CA 95642; 800-841-1072 or 209-223-3500; FAX 209-223-1299. Internet: http://www.gatehouseinn.com. E-mail: info@gatehouse inn.com.

The Kennedy Mine (1856) and its tailings wheels, which dominate the landscape north and east of Jackson, is 0.25 mile east of the Gate House Inn on Jackson Gate Road. These giant wheels, considered engineering marvels when constructed in 1905, were erected to move tailings from the Kennedy Mine over a hill into a tailing pond across Jackson Gate Road. There is a trail to an overlook of the first and second tailing wheels (the latter has collapsed to the ground) and the Kennedy Mine Headframe. The third tailing wheel is up the hill in Kennedy Wheels

Downtown Jackson is a blend of old and new in the historic section of town.

Park. The nearby Argonaut Mine, first operated in 1850, was closed during World War II. Both mines reached depths of more than 5,000 feet.

Jackson has a number of motels, bed and breakfast inns, and restaurants, which make it an ideal place to stay overnight.

Side trips from Jackson begin on CA 88 to reach Chaw'Se Indian Grinding Rock State Historic Park, Volcano, Daffodil Hill and Silver Lake. Proceed north for 6 miles to Groveland and turn left on the Groveland-Volcano Road to Chaw'Se Indian Grinding Rock State Historic Park.

CHAW'SE INDIAN GRINDING ROCK STATE HISTORIC PARK

Chaw'se Indian Grinding Rock State Historic Park, between Volcano and Pine Grove, is the best presentation of Indian culture and history in California's Gold Rush Country. Among the recreations and numerous artifacts is the largest collection of bedrock mortars in North America. Within the 135-acre park, in the meadow just below the visitors center, more than 1,185 chaw-ses (mortar cups) and numerous Indian drawings cover a large, flat rock. The local Indians used these mortar cups to grind up acorns, a staple in their diet.

A recreated Miwok Village, complete with full size roundhouse, is nearby. Chaw'Se Regional Indian Museum, which features extensive exhibits of basketry, feather regalia, jewelry, arrowpoints and tools used by

The Kennedy Mine and tailing wheels dominate the landscape north of Jackson.

JACKSON—UPPER

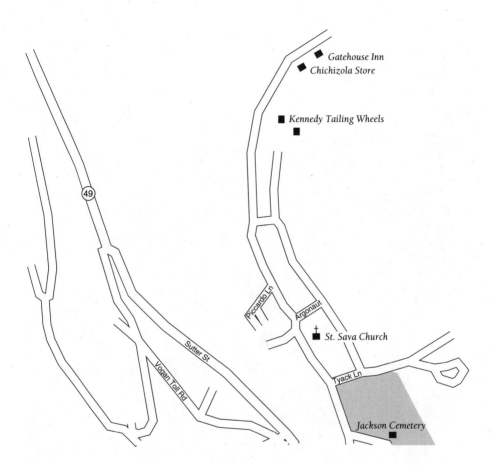

the Miwok and other Sierra Nevada Native American groups, is housed in a 2 story building near the park's entrance. Chaw'Se Indian Grinding Rock State Historic Park, 14481 Pine Grove-Volcano Road, Pine Grove, CA 95665; 209-296-7488. Open daylight hours; camping; fee is $5 per vehicle. The Chaw'Se Regional Indian Museum is open from 11 A.M. to 3 P.M., weekdays, and 10 A.M. to 4 P.M. on Saturday and Sunday.

This area was extensively mined by the 49ers during the Gold Rush.

Proceed 2 miles north on the Pine Grove-Volcano Road to Volcano.

VOLCANO

Volcano, populated by some 100 people, is set in what appears to be the remnants of a volcanic caldera. On the east side of Main Street, only 2 history packed blocks long, are Gold Rush buildings. On the west side only stone facades hint at structures from the past. Volcano has retained much of its historic appearance. While some may look at Volcano as a virtually deserted community, locals see it as a quiet, close knit community. Volcano is quaint, somewhat quiet, but well worth the drive off CA 49.

The magnificent 3 story St. George Hotel (1862) was preceded by 2 other structures dating to 1850. The hotel is 1 of only a few historic 3 story structures remaining in California's Gold Rush Country, and according to its advertisement, was "the tallest and most elegant hotel existing in the Mother Lode" when it was built. The St. George Hotel stands majestically at the southern edge of town and remains 1 of the most elegant of the historic hotels in California's Gold Rush Country. The bar is authentic to the original structure. The rooms are attractively decorated and furnished in sparse style indicative of the era. St. George Hotel, 2 Main Street, P.O. Box 9, Volcano, CA 95689; Telephone and FAX: 209-296-4458.

According to a plaque on the wall of The Country Store in the middle of central Volcano, a general store has operated on its site continuously since 1852. While the store now sports a deli along with the staples, much of the character of the past can still be seen here. The Country Store, 16146 Main Street, P.O. Box 156, Volcano, CA 95689 209-296-4459. Hours: Monday through Saturday, 10 A.M. to 6 P.M., and Sunday, 11 A.M. to 5 P.M.

The Volcano Theatre Company, 1 of several active playhouse groups in Amador County, operates from the Cobblestone Theatre. The façade of the VTC's stage is all that remains of the stone storefront from the original structure that housed Adolph Meyer's Tobacco & Cigar Emporium (1856) and, after it burned in 1900, the Lavezzo's Wine Shop. Volcano Theatre Company, P.O. Box 88, Volcano, CA 95689.

DAFFODIL HILL

Daffodil Hill, a springtime color extravaganza and a local tradition, is located 3 miles north of Volcano on Rams Horn Grade Road at the intersection of Shake Ridge Road. Amador County pioneers Arthur and Lizzie Van Vorst McLaughlin established the McLaughlin Ranch in 1877 at this location. They bought the land from an old Dutchman, Pete Denzer, who had planted daffodils around the home site from bulbs that he had brought with him from his native Holland.

The daffodils soon became Lizzie's most prized possessions as she worked to increase the size of her daffodil garden. Her work is carried on

Hotel guests get an excellent view of Volcano's historic park from the third floor of the St. George Hotel.

today by her grandchildren, Arthur Lucot and Mary Lucot Ryan and their families, who open up the old farm every spring. There are 6 acres planted in daffodils with 300 varieties and an estimated 400,000 blooms each spring. Adding to the color of the flowers, peacocks, and peahens roam the grounds. Picnic tables are available. Hours are daily, 10 A.M. to 5 P.M., weather permitting, from about mid-March until mid-April. Donations are used to plant more daffodils. For information, call 209-223-0608.

For those who are going up into the mountains, the 40-mile drive from Jackson on CA 88 offers numerous sweeping vistas and opportunities to see where the 49ers crossed the Sierra Nevada at Carson Pass. Silver Lake, just below the western side of 8,650-foot Carson Pass, has ties to the Gold Rush.

SILVER LAKE

Plasse's Resort (1853) is steeped in history. Operated by descendants of its founder, Ramon Pierre Plasse, this tent and RV resort is located at 7,200 feet just off CA 88, and just below the famous Mormon Immigrant Trail. The original cabin (1853) is preserved on site. Silver Lake is surrounded by 8,000- and 9,000-foot peaks crossed by 49ers and other emigrants who followed California's Trail. Contact Plasse's Resort, 30001 Plasse Road, Silver Lake, CA 95666; 209-258-8814. June through September.

Return to CA 49 either at Jackson or from Pine Grove, via Ridge Road to Sutter Creek.

SUTTER CREEK

Sutter Creek was named for John A. Sutter, who first visited here in 1846 and later prospected in the nearby creeks in 1848. Sutter Creek is one of the most picturesque of the gold mining towns in California's Gold Rush Country. The town's historic buildings line Highway 49.

Sutter Creek was the site of the Old Eureka Mine, one of the most lucrative in the area. Leland J. Stanford, best known as the founder of Stanford University, Governor of California and co-builder of the Central Pacific Railroad, made much of his fortune from his investment in the Lincoln Mine which was located just north of Sutter Creek.

The Bellotti Inn of Sutter Creek (1858) is considered to be the oldest continuously operating inn in California's Gold Rush Country. The Bellotti Inn of Sutter Creek, 53 Main Street, Sutter Creek, CA 95685; 209-267-5211.

The Sutter Creek Inn (1859), originally constructed as a prefab house, was renovated in 1882 and has been expanded since 1966 to its current size. A popular Gold Rush Country inn and my personal favorite, The Sutter Creek Inn's 16 rooms make an ideal location for a romantic weekend. The grounds, along with its trademark ducks, are especially attractive in the spring and summer when flowers blossom. The Sutter

Sutter Creek Inn.

SUTTER CREEK

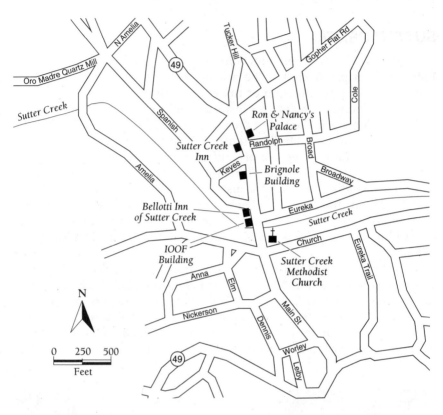

Creek Inn, 75 Main Street, Sutter Creek, CA 95685; 209-267-5606. Internet address: http://www.suttercreekinn.com; E-mail: info@ suttercreekinn.com.

Ron and Nancy's Palace, across from The Sutter Creek Inn, occupies a saloon building that dates to 1897. This restaurant has the appearance and atmosphere of the Gold Rush. Ron and Nancy's Palace, 76 Main Street, Sutter Creek, CA 95685; 209-267-1355.

WALKING TOUR OF SUTTER CREEK

Central Sutter Creek is 5 blocks long by 2 blocks wide and is an excellent town for walking. Most, but not all, of the historic structures are along Main Street (CA 49). Significant structures include the Brignole Building (1856) at the intersection of Keyes Street and Main Street, the I.O.O.F. building (1865) adjacent to the Bellotti Inn and the Sutter Creek Methodist Church (1862).

Continue north on CA 49 for 3 miles to Amador City.

Mine House Inn and downtown Amador City.

AMADOR CITY

Amador City is considered to be the state's smallest incorporated city, both in population (210 residents) and size (about 1 block long). It lives up to its reputation in size but don't pass it up for this reason. The town was named for José Maria Amador who mined here in 1848. With the discovery of gold bearing quartz, the Keystone Mine, whose headframe still stands above Amador City, began operations in 1853.

On the west side of CA 49, 100 yards south of central Amador City, is the Mine House Inn. The building was originally the headquarters for the Keystone Mine. Of the 7 sleeping rooms, my favorite is The Vault Room, complete with the original walk-in safe which housed gold bullion before the gold was shipped to San Francisco. Mine House Inn, 14125 Highway 49, P.O. Box 245, Amador City, CA 95601; 209-267-5900 or 800-646-3473.

The large frame building on the east side of CA 49 is the Amador Hotel (1855) which houses modern shops. The Imperial Hotel (1879) a bed and breakfast and restaurant, at the northern end of Amador City, has a good restaurant. The Imperial Hotel, 14202 Highway 49, P.O. Box 195, Amador City, CA 95601; 209-267-9172 or 800-242-5594.

Continue north on CA 49 for 3 miles to Drytown.

DRYTOWN

At Drytown, the old brick building (1850s) on the west side of CA 49, which houses an antique store, is reported to have been used by William Randolph Hearst's father, George Hearst. He operated a printing press and maintained his mining office in this building. Continue north on CA 49 for 5 miles to Plymouth.

PLYMOUTH

Plymouth is a post-Gold Rush town. A number of services are available, including restaurants, motels, RV facilities and gasoline. Plymouth serves as the gateway to the Shenandoah Valley. Turn east on County Highway E-16 and go 1 mile to the intersection of Fiddletown Road. To get to Fiddletown, go straight ahead for 5 miles. To visit the Shenandoah Valley and the Amador County wine country, turn left and drive 3 miles.

FIDDLETOWN

Fiddletown was settled in 1849 by miners from Missouri who were known to play their fiddles when they were not mining. Bret Harte's "An Episode in Fiddletown" was set here. The Fiddletown General Store, on Main Street, has been operating continuously since 1853. On display and "for sale," appropriately, are many kinds of fiddles. According to owner

Fiddletown General Store.

Chinese rammed earth adobe at Fiddletown.

Reid Mackey, an old fashioned music jam for fiddlers and others is held either on the front porch (if weather is good) or inside the store every Sunday afternoon from 3 P.M. to 6 P.M. Everyone is welcome to bring their fiddle and join in the fun. The Fiddletown General Store, 14458 Fiddletown Road, P.O. Box 237, Fiddletown, CA 95629; 209-245-3671. Monday through Saturday, 10 A.M. to 6 P.M., Sunday, Noon to 6 P.M.

Across the street from the Fiddletown General Store is the imposing 2 story Schallhorn Building (1870), which served as a stagecoach stop.

One of the few remaining rammed earth adobes in California's Gold Rush Country is at the corner of Fiddletown Road and Jibboom Street. The adobe was built in the early 1850s and was as the home of several Chinese doctors. The building now serves as a museum of Chinese artifacts. Hours: April through October, Saturdays, 12 P.M. to 4 P.M. Other historic buildings in Fiddletown include the restored Fiddletown Schoolhouse (1852) and the Farnham residence (early 1850s).

When you have completed your tour of Fiddletown, return via Fiddletown Road to County Road E-16. Turn right and enter the scenic Shenandoah Valley, home of the Amador County wine country.

FIDDLETOWN/SHENANDOAH

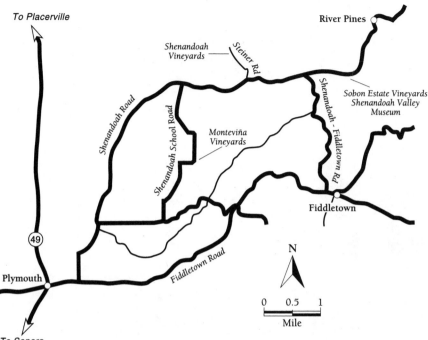

SHENANDOAH VALLEY AND THE AMADOR WINE COUNTRY

The Shenandoah Valley, home to 11 wineries, is thought to have been named by prospectors from Virginia for the famous valley in their native state. The oldest, the D'Agostini Winery, is now operated as the Sobon Estate Vineyards by Lee Sobon. Founded in 1856 by the Uhlinger family, who emigrated from Switzerland, the winery passed to the D'Agostini family in 1911. Sobon uses wine tanks in the fermenting process which were coopered by Jacob Uhlinger from oak trees native to the Shenandoah Valley. The Shenandoah Valley Museum, incorporated into the original stone cellar constructed by Uhlinger, displays tools used in early wine making. Sobon Estate Vineyards, 14430 Shenandoah Road, Plymouth, CA 95669; 209-245-6554. Hours: daily, 10 A.M. to 5 P.M.; closed Thanksgiving, Christmas and New Years Day.

There are signs throughout the area which direct visitors to the dozen vineyards in the area. Personal favorites include the Shenandoah Vineyards (try their Cabernet), 12300 Steiner Road, Plymouth, CA 95669; 209-245-4455 and Monteviña Vineyards (excellent Zinfandel), 20680 Shenandoah School Road, Plymouth, CA 95669; 209-245-6942.

After you have completed your tour of the Shenandoah Valley, return to CA 49 and proceed north to El Dorado County. Diamond Springs is the first stop in this 19-mile drive through gently rolling countryside.

AMADOR COUNTY TRAVEL INFORMATION

AMADOR COUNTY CHAMBER OF COMMERCE
Telephone: 800-649-4988 or 209-223-0350; FAX 209-223-4465
Mailing Address: P.O. Box 596, Jackson, CA 95642
Street Address: 125 Peek Street, Suite B
Internet: http//www.cdepot.net/chamber

Monteviña Vineyards.

Chapter Ten

MONO COUNTY

A SIDE TRIP TO BODIE STATE HISTORIC PARK

A trip to Mono County and Bodie is a distant side trip from CA 49 involving at least 1 hard day or 2 more relaxed days of driving and sightseeing. Perhaps the most logical way to visit Bodie, for those driving in or out of California from the east, is to schedule a visit here at the beginning or ending of a trip to California.

One of the more logical points of departure from CA 49 for Mono County is CA 88 from Jackson (See Amador County, page 92) through Alpine County to CA 89 and Bridgeport on US 395. Total driving distance each way is 165 miles. While this may sound easy at 65 miles per hour on an interstate highway, these roads are two lanes and there are 3 passes to negotiate (Carson at 8,650 feet, Monitor at 8,314 feet, and Devils Gate at 7,519 feet). Allow 6 hours to drive each way. Because this route covers some of the prettiest areas and offers numerous vistas as you cross the Sierra Nevada, additional time might be desired to allow for stops to take in the magnificent scenery

Plan to spend time at the summits of each pass and at Marklee, the county seat of Alpine County and the smallest county seat of the least populated county in California. From Carson Pass east through Hope Valley along the Carson River to Woodfords, CA 88 parallels and crosses the Mormon Emigrant Trail followed by 49ers on their way to the gold fields of the western slopes of the Sierra Nevada. Woodfords is the site of one of the stops on the Pony Express Route.

BRIDGEPORT/BODIE

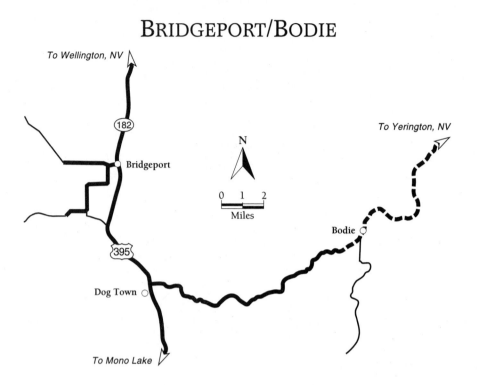

To Wellington, NV

182

To Yerington, NV

Bridgeport

N

Bodie

0 1 2
Miles

395

Dog Town

To Mono Lake

BRIDGEPORT

Bridgeport, the closest town to Bodie, is 20 miles north and the county seat of Mono County. The Mono County Courthouse (1880) is the dominant building in town. Motels, restaurants, and gasoline are available in Bridgeport. Proceed south on US 395 for 7 miles to CA 270. Bodie is 12 miles from US 395. The last mile of roadway into Bodie is dirt and gravel.

BODIE STATE HISTORIC PARK

Named for Waterman S. Body (or William S. Bodey) who found gold here in 1859, Bodie is the best known "ghost town" in California's Gold Rush Country. Incorporated into the Bodie State Historic Park in 1962, is maintained in a state of "arrested decay." By 1880, there were 10,000 people in Bodie, and the town was well known for frequent killings and wickedness. It is reported that one young girl, upon learning that she was going to Bodie with her family, wrote: "Good bye God, I'm going to Bodie."

One hundred sixty-eight buildings, all that remain from the several hundred built, are in various states of deterioration at Bodie. The dry air of the high Sierra Nevada has helped slow the rate of decay of the buildings. Most buildings are closed to visitors but those few that are open allow a glimpse at past life in Bodie. The old Standard Mine facility, its stamping mills silenced many years ago, is closed to the public.

The only services available at Bodie State Historic Park are toilets and potable water. The park is open from sunrise to sunset. Even though the park is open in the winter, the road is not plowed, so access may be limited to snowmobiles, skis, or snowshoes when there is snowfall. Winter visits should be carefully planned with potential severe weather changes considered. Fee: $5 per vehicle. Bodie State Historic Park, P.O. Box 515, Bridgeport, CA 93517; 619-647-6445.

MONO COUNTY TRAVEL INFORMATION

Telephone: 800-GO-CALIF (462-2543)

Chapter   Eleven

EL DORADO COUNTY

El Dorado is Spanish for the "golden one." The name is fitting for the area since James W. Marshall made his discovery of gold at Sutter's Mill in what became El Dorado County. This entire region proved to be rich in gold. Today, El Dorado County, founded in 1850, is rich in agricultural pursuits. Apple orchards and vineyards are dominant features on the hillsides of El Dorado County. The gentle hills of the southern Sierra Nevada counties are replaced with steep slopes of canyon walls and higher mountains of the northern Sierra Nevada in El Dorado County. Wildlife, including deer, turkey, and other small animals, can frequently be seen.

Even though Marshall Gold Discovery State Historic Park is the most significant historic site in El Dorado County (See Chapter Four, page 31), there are a number of other Gold Rush sites for visitors to explore.

Diamond Springs, 3 miles south of Placerville, takes its name from a spring so clear that the 49ers thought that the water sparkled like diamonds. The I.O.O.F. building (1859) is 2 blocks north of CA 49 on Odd Fellows Road.

Continue north on CA 49 for 2 miles to an overlook of Placerville. Drive slowly down the hill and you can get a good view of Placerville. Follow CA 49 and turn right on Main Street.

PLACERVILLE

Placerville has been known by several names since its founding in 1848. The town was first called Old Dry Diggins. After local citizens took

EL DORADO COUNTY

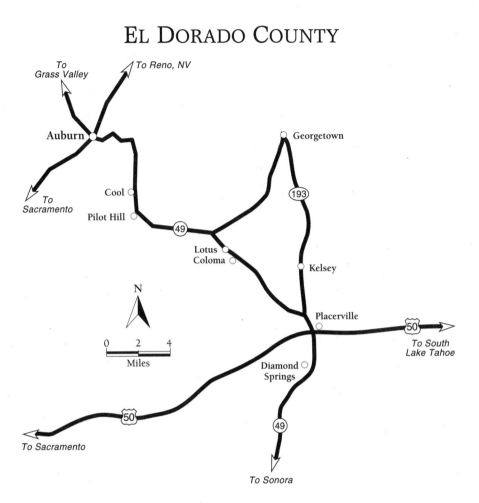

To Grass Valley

To Reno, NV

Auburn

Georgetown

To Sacramento

Cool

Pilot Hill

(193)

(49)

Lotus

Coloma

Kelsey

N

0   2   4

Miles

Placerville

(50)

To South Lake Tahoe

Diamond Springs

(50)

To Sacramento

(49)

To Sonora

law and order into their own hands and hung 3 men in 1849, the town became known as Hangtown. In May 1854, in an effort to improve the town's image, the name was changed to Placerville.

The region around Placerville was rich in gold. Coloma is just 8 miles from Placerville. Hangtown Creek, which runs through downtown Placerville, yielded large quantities of gold. Placerville was both an important gold mining town and a distribution point for towns and camps to the north and south.

John Mohler Studebaker, a blacksmith, arrived in Placerville in 1853. He spent the next 5 years earning his gold by making and selling wheelbarrows, shovels, picks, and other mining related tools. He took his fortune earned in California's Gold Rush Country, invested it with brothers Henry and Clement and helped build the Studebaker Company into a major vehicle manufacturing concern (first wagons, then cars and trucks).

PLACERVILLE OVERVIEW

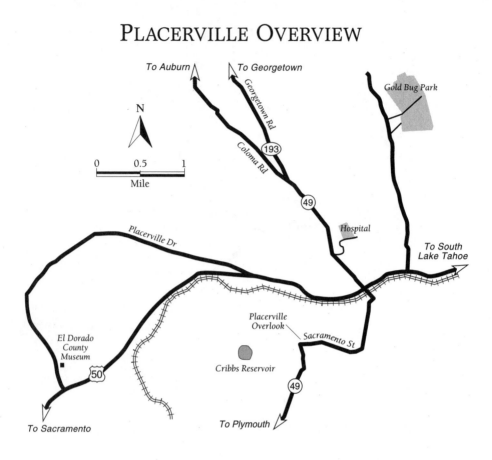

HANGTOWN FRY

Despite the efforts of its citizens to eliminate the name Hangtown, the legacy of that era remains. One of the most enduring edible delicacy of the Gold Rush is the Hangtown Fry, a world-renowned omelet.

Although there are many versions of its origin, the most credible story tells that a miner, laden with gold from a recent find in 1849, demanded that the cook at the El Dorado Hotel prepare the "finest and most expensive meal in the house." The most expensive items were eggs, bacon, and oysters which the cook quickly put together for the hungry miner. The Hangtown Fry was born and endures today. For those who want to try this dish at home, try the recipe below. The Hangtown Fry is available throughout California's Gold Rush Country.

The real life story of the legendary "Snowshoe" Thompson is as enduring as the Hangtown Fry. Until the railroad arrived in Placerville in 1868, the only way to get mail across the Sierra Nevada was by man and beast.

Placerville, early 1850.

In 1855, the only carrier on the job quit when his mule froze to death in a blizzard. Mail destined for the eastern states began to accumulate in the Placerville post office.

HANGTOWN FRY RECIPE

Ingredients: 1 egg, beaten with 1 tablespoon of milk; breading mixture of cracker and bread crumbs; oil; 3 oysters; 2 slices of bacon; and 2 eggs.

Preparation: Dip the oysters in the beaten egg and then into the breading mixture. Pan fry the oysters until three-fourths cooked. At the same time, in a separate skillet, fry the bacon until almost crisp. Beat the eggs lightly. Place the 2 bacon pieces parallel and off center in a fry pan. Pour a small amount of the eggs over the bacon. Place the oysters on the bacon and pour the remainder of the eggs over the bacon and oysters. Cook and then fold the omelet over the oysters. Place a lid over the skillet and cook until the steam blends together the flavors and simmers the omelet until done. Makes 1 serving. *Recipe courtesy Doug Noble and the El Dorado Chamber of Commerce.*

A 28-year-old Norwegian by the name of John Thompson offered to carry the mail to Genoa, near Carson City, Nevada, every 2 weeks no matter what the weather. Even though the postmaster did not have the authority to hire or pay him, Thompson took on the job of getting the mail across the Sierra Nevada by himself.

Thompson used snowshoes for the 2-day trip to the top and used his long snow skis to make the downhill run in one day. He never failed to complete a trip, but he never received a payment for his work because the Placerville postmaster could not pay him. Despite traveling to Washington, D.C., and petitioning Congress, he was never paid for his services by the government.

Local citizens, grateful for his service, raised money for him to buy a small ranch near Genoa. A monument commemorating his efforts stands in Placerville at the intersection of Main and Sacramento streets. Another monument is at Carson Pass and his snowshoes are on display at the Plumas Eureka State Park Museum (See Plumas County, page 193).

Placerville has an abundance of modern hotels, motels, bed & breakfasts, RV facilities, and restaurants which make the area a natural overnight stop. Placerville is on US 50, a major road leading to mountain resorts and Lake Tahoe.

TOURING PLACERVILLE

The best place to being your tour of central Placerville is in front of the Hangman's Tree Bar and Cafe Sarah located at 301-305 Main Street on the north side of the street. The Hangman's Tree Bar is directly over the site of the Hangman's Tree which was used to hang 3 men in 1849. The historic district continues east for 3 blocks. Specific sites to be seen include the City Hall at 487 and 489 Main Street. The red building was the Confidence Engine Company Hall, the town's fire station from 1860 and the site of many of early Placerville's dances and balls. The yellow

PLACERVILLE

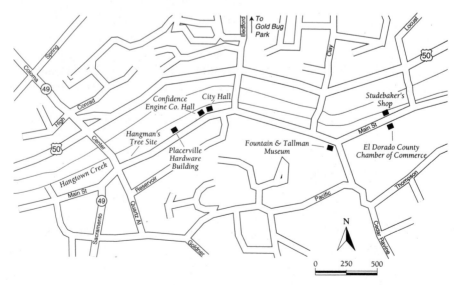

Placerville City Hall Building.

building, built originally in 1861, was known as the Emigrant Jane Building for an early emigrant named Mary Jane Shoyers. She reportedly drove a herd of horses across the plains to Placerville. She sold the horses and made enough to build the Emigrant Jane Building.

Studebaker's shop, from 1853 to 1858, was located at 543 Main Street, across from the El Dorado County Chamber of Commerce, at 542 Main Street. The Cary House, where Horace Greeley addressed miners and businessmen alike in 1859, stood at 300 Main Street on the site of the current Raffles Hotel. Placerville Hardware Building (1856), oldest hardware store in the west, stands at 441-443 Main Street. Today the building houses the Pioneer Hardware.

There are 3 museums in Placerville. The Fountain-Tallman Soda Works Building (1853 or 1854), with 2-foot walls, housed a soda pop manufacturing business. The Fountain & Tallman Museum, 524 Main Street, Placerville, CA 95667; 916-626-0773. Hours: Summer months, Friday through Sunday, Noon to 4 P.M., and winter months, Saturday and Sunday, Noon to 4 P.M. The El Dorado County Historical Museum, 100 Placerville Drive, Placerville, CA 95667; 916-621-5865. Hours: Wednesday through Saturday, 10 A.M. to 4 P.M., and Sunday, Noon to 4 P.M.

Hangtown's Gold Bug Park, located 0.9 mile north of US 50 on Bedford Avenue, is operated by the City of Placerville. This 61-acre park was an active mining area where more than 250 individual mines were in operation. The principal exhibits area is grouped around the Gold Bug Mine building, which houses an 8-stamp mill and other displays. Gold Bug Park, Bedford Avenue, Placerville; 916-642-5238. Hours: 10 A.M. to 4 P.M., daily.

In the tradition of its agricultural heritage, Placerville and El Dorado County celebrates Apple Days from Labor Day through October on Apple Hill. Fall harvest produce is found at numerous farms along a clearly marked trail. The Boeger Winery uses a stone cellar built in 1857 as its tasting room. Visitors can picnic on the beautifully landscaped grounds, which are especially lovely in the spring. The Boeger Winery, 1709 Carson Road, Placerville, CA 95667; 916-622-8094; FAX 209-622-8112.

A side trip to Georgetown is a must if time permits. Continue north 1 mile from central Placerville on CA 49. Take CA 193 to the right for 15 miles. Within a mile, CA 193 begins the descent down to the South Fork of the American River. This is an especially scenic drive in the spring, when the hillsides are covered with poppies and other flowers, and in the fall, when the trees along the roadside are colored with yellows and oranges. At Kelsey, on the left, are the remains of the old blacksmith shop that James W. Marshall operated just prior to his death.

GEORGETOWN

Georgetown's Main Street literally sets the town apart from other Gold Rush towns. Georgetown was first established in 1849 and called

Stamp mill at Hangtown's Gold Bug Park.

GEORGETOWN/PLACERVILLE

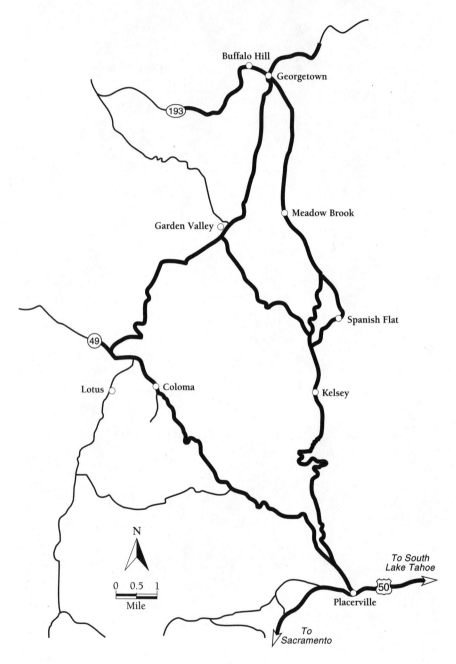

Buffalo Hill

Georgetown

193

Meadow Brook

Garden Valley

Spanish Flat

49

Lotus

Coloma

Kelsey

N

0   0.5   1
Mile

To South
Lake Tahoe

50

Placerville

To
Sacramento

GEORGETOWN

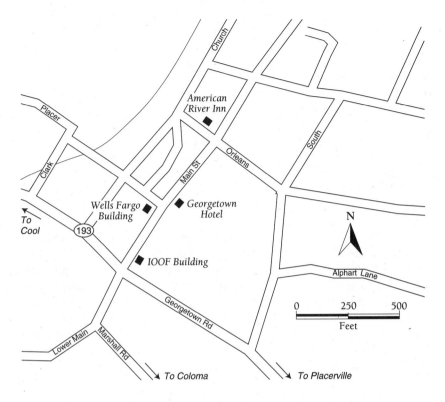

Growlersburg. After fire destroyed Growlersburg in 1852, the town was rebuilt as Georgetown. To reduce the chance of another fire destroying the entire town, Georgetown's main street was built 100 feet wide, wider than any other street in California's Gold Rush Country.

Georgetown is known as the "Pride of the Mountains." The clear air, its beautiful mountain setting, and stately trees make Georgetown a favorite tourist destination. Numerous fruit trees planted by the 49ers thrive today. At fall foliage season, Georgetown is especially pretty when the trees are colored brightly.

TOURING GEORGETOWN

The Georgetown Hotel (1896), on Main Street, besides having rooms to let, has the best restaurant in town. Call 916-333-2848. The I.O.O.F. Hall (1869) is still used for local social activities. The Wells, Fargo & Company building (1852), across the wide Main Street from the I.O.O.F. building, is now a cafe. At the northern end of Main Street at Orleans

Street is the elegant American River Inn (1899), which replaced the original American Hotel (circa 1853). Call 800-245-6566 or 916-333-4499.

Return to CA 49 by retracing your drive on CA 193 or take Marshall Grade Road from central Georgetown through Garden Valley to Lotus, a distance of 12 miles. This road descends into the American River valley and provides a spectacular overview of the area. The Sierra Nevada House (1850), at the intersection of CA 49 and Lotus Road (on the south bank of the South Fork of the American River), is reported to be haunted. I didn't stay long enough to see any ghosts but there are plenty of stories about them. Lotus was originally named Marshall in honor of James W. Marshall. Coloma is 0.75 mile south on CA 49.

After visiting Coloma (See Chapter Four, Where the Gold Rush Began, page 28), proceed north on CA 49 toward Auburn. Some of the largest and most stately oak trees of any along CA 49 are found in this area. With huge trunks and spreading wide, they stand majestic as they did when Marshall found gold nearby.

The Bayley House is located 1 mile north of Pilot Hill, which was named for the beacon fires built to guide travelers coming valley below. The Bayley House is one of the more unusual architectural sights found along CA 49 and in California's Gold Rush Country. The large, imposing building made of bricks with large plantation house styled columns (since fallen down), is located on the west side of CA 49. Alcandor A. Bayley, who had the hotel building constructed in 1862, mistakenly believed that the railroad would pass nearby and the hotel would serve the needs of passengers. The old house is in a steady state of decline and not open to the public. Four miles beyond the Bayley House is the small village of Cool. There is a "stop" sign here and a few stores.

Just 0.5 mile farther, CA 49 begins a series of switchbacks that lead to and over the American River. The climb up from the river is in Placer County and leads to central Auburn in just 4 miles.

EL DORADO COUNTY TRAVEL INFORMATION

EL DORADO COUNTY CHAMBER OF COMMERCE
Telephone: 800-457-6279 or 916-621-5885; FAX 916-642-1624
Mailing Address and Street Address, 542 Main Street, Placerville, CA 95667

C h a p t e r   T w e l v e

PLACER COUNTY

A significant number of the Placer County gold mining camps on the North, Middle, and South forks of the American River are buried deep beneath the waters of Folsom Lake State Recreation Area. Among these is Mormon Island, site of discovery of gold by Mormons who were employed by John A. Sutter to build a flour mill. Sam Brannan, who started the Gold Rush in San Francisco, was given gold nuggets by the Mormons who mined here shortly after Marshall's discovery at nearby Sutter's Mill. The nuggets that he held high as he walked the streets of San Francisco on May 12, 1848, yelling out, "Gold, gold, gold, from the American River," were from Mormon Island and not Sutter's Mill.

Few areas of California's Gold Rush Country rival the scenic beauty found in the rugged canyons and divides of Shirt Tail Canyon, the Middle Fork of the American River, and the Rubicon River. While the rewards were high in this gold rich area, the 49ers experienced great hardships traveling over the divides and into the canyons. Thanks to a network of good roads, today's visitors can travel in relative ease to many of these sites by automobile.

Leland J. Stanford, founder of Stanford University, toiled in his store from 1853 through 1855 at Michigan Bluff, on the spectacular bluffs overlooking the Middle Fork of the American River. He reportedly waited on the 49ers during the day and slept on the counter of the store at night.

Huge oak trees grace Big Oak Flat, near Foresthill and high above the Middle Fork of the American River. James W. Marshall is reported to have prospected for gold here in 1850. Deadwood, first mined in 1852

Placer County

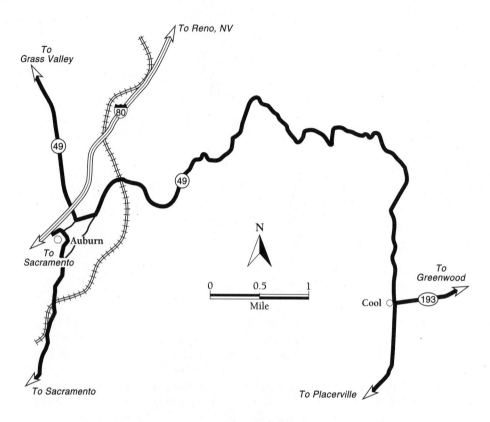

and located only 7 miles from Michigan Bluff, overlooks the spectacular El Dorado Canyon above the North Fork of the Middle Fork of the American River. The only reminder of Deadwood is a small cemetery at the end of a road that is typically passable only by four-wheel-drive vehicles.

Placer County stretches from the Sacramento Valley to Lake Tahoe and the Nevada–California State Line. CA 49 crosses Placer County in only 15 miles. This distance, however, contains most of the traffic lights and the only 4-lane highway on the entire length of CA 49. There are no traffic lights on CA 49 north of Placer County.

There are many modern hotels, motels, bed & breakfasts, RV facilities, and restaurants in Auburn, making the area a natural overnight stop.

I-80, the major east-west highway in northern California, connecting San Francisco and Sacramento with Reno, passes through much of Placer County. The interstate highway has replaced US 40, the Lincoln Highway, but there are still fragments of that famous highway visible near Truckee.

Placer County Courthouse Museum.

AUBURN

The mines at Auburn proved to be among the richest in all of California's Gold Rush Country, particularly those in Auburn Ravine. Gold was first found here by Claude Chana on May 16, 1848. Chana, who owned property on the nearby Bear River, was on his way to Sutter's Mill with a group of Frenchmen and native Indians to mine for gold. When they stopped to camp overnight, Chana tested the gravel in Auburn Ravine and found 3 large nuggets. He decided to stay here and mine. Chana, immortalized with a large statue at the entrance to Old Town Auburn, went on to found the still-flourishing fruit industry in the area.

Important as a gold mining town, Auburn also served as a regional transportation center. The magnificent Placer County Courthouse (1894) at Auburn, the dominant feature of the downtown area, replaced a wooden building built in 1853. First called Wood's Dry Diggins in 1849, Auburn's Old Town now boasts a number of Gold Rush buildings dating to 1852 including California's oldest post office. Located in The Plaza, in central Old Town Auburn, the Auburn Post Office has been in continuous operation since its founding in 1852. A strip of old buildings on the east side of Sacramento Street is known as the Chinese Merchant's section. On nearby Commercial Street, antique stores are housed on Lawyer's Row in buildings first constructed in 1852 and replaced after the fire of 1858. The 3-story Auburn Hook and Ladder Company Fire House Number Two (1893) houses Auburn's fire company, which was established in 1852.

AUBURN

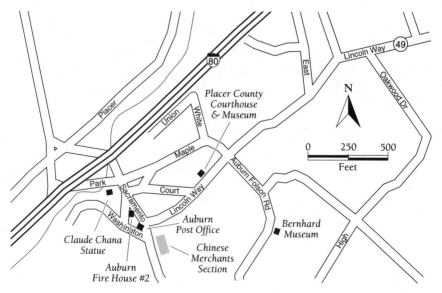

FOREST HILL OVERVIEW

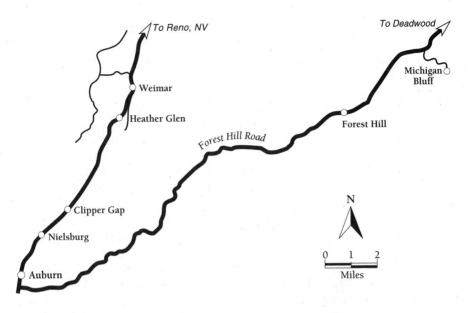

Auburn is home to a number of excellent museums including the Placer County Museum, housed in the County Courthouse, and the Bernhard Museum housed in the oldest remaining wooden structure in Placer County (1851). Placer Country Museum, 101 Maple Street, Auburn, CA 95603; 916-889-6500. Hours: Tuesday through Sunday, 10 A.M. to 4 P.M. Entry fee. Bernhard Museum, 291 Auburn-Folsom Road, Auburn, CA 95603; 916-889-4156. Hours: Tuesday through Friday, 11 A.M. to 3 P.M., Saturday and Sunday, Noon to 4 P.M.

SIDE TRIP TO FORESTHILL, DEADWOOD, MICHIGAN BLUFF, AND THE MIDDLE FORK OF THE AMERICAN RIVER

A side trip to Foresthill and the surrounding high country and steep canyons in the summer or fall is one of the more rewarding trips in California's Gold Rush Country. The scenery is spectacular so plan on a full day in this area if you travel beyond Foresthill. Bring your camera and plenty of film.

The round trip from Auburn to Foresthill is an easy 1-hour drive. Allow an additional 3 hours for a drive to Deadwood and Michigan Bluff. Oak Tree Flat and the Middle Fork of the American River area require three hours of driving. Add additional time to take in the magnificent scenery regardless of which side trip you take.

Before visiting Deadwood, Michigan Bluff, and/or Oak Tree Flat, plan for food, water, and gasoline. There are several restaurants, one grocery store, one gasoline station, and several stores specializing in hunting and camping supplies in Foresthill. There are no public vehicle service facilities beyond Foresthill. Check your fuel level before departing from Foresthill in any direction. There is a Chevron station on the west side of Foresthill.

From Auburn, take the Foresthill Road for 15 miles to Foresthill. This drive, along the narrow ridge known as the Foresthill Divide that separates the North Fork and the Middle Fork of the American River, follows the Middle Fork much of the distance with several spectacular vistas.

The Langstaff Building (1858), on the north side on Main Street in Foresthill, is the oldest in town. One block away from the Langstaff Building on Harrison Street is the Foresthill Divide Museum. Foresthill Divide Museum, 24601 Harrison Street, Foresthill, CA 95631; 916-367-3988. Open May through October Wednesdays, Saturdays and Sundays, Noon to 4 P.M.

If you are in Foresthill at the time of fall foliage, drive to Church Street 1 block south of Main Street. The house on the left with the white picket fence is surrounded by colorful maples and sweet gum trees reminiscent of scenery in New England.

Michigan Bluff and Deadwood can be reached by continuing on Foresthill Road along the Foresthill Divide. In order to see both locales

Langstaff Building.

FOREST HILL

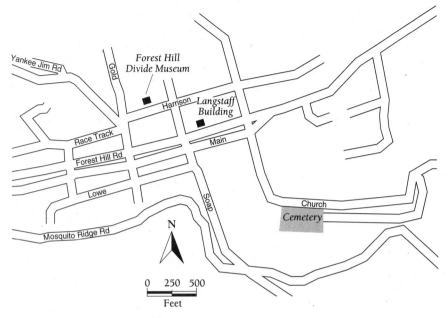

and enjoy the spectacular scenery, drive 24 miles on the Foresthill Road to Deadwood Road. Deadwood Road is a dirt road which receives little or no maintenance. In the summer and fall, the Deadwood Road can be negotiated in a four-wheel-drive vehicle, pickup or, depending on the condition of the road, by sedan. Inquire in Foresthill before you attempt this road in a sedan. Winter and spring travel on Deadwood Road is best not attempted when the snow is deep.

Follow the Deadwood Road along the Deadwood Ridge for 15 miles. There are a number of vistas in the last 5 miles, particularly where the road narrows and hugs the edge of the canyon wall. Drive to the sign that reads "Deadwood Cemetery".

Walk 100 yards up the rise to the cemetery. This area was once a mining camp. The cemetery site and a few grave markers are all that remain of this busy camp. Take time while here to contemplate the desolate beauty, the river canyon below, and the difficulty miners and their horses must have had in traveling the 7 miles (as the crow flies) down the canyon to Michigan Bluff. Return to the Foresthill Road and drive west toward Foresthill. At 6 miles from Foresthill, turn left on Michigan Bluff Road. The drive to Michigan Bluff on a paved road is relatively uneventful until you reach the bluff overlooking the Middle Fork of the American River. Perched several thousand fee above the American River, you can easily imagine the difficulty that miners experienced in getting to Michigan Bluff. Only a few houses from the early twentieth century remain here. The view, however, is spectacular as the mountainside literally drops away before you in a breathtaking view of the American River Canyon.

Return to Foresthill if you are planning to drive back to Auburn, CA 49, or I-80.

If Oak Tree Flat and the spectacular vistas of the Middle Fork of the American River are on your itinerary, go south (literally, down the hill) on Gorman Ranch Road about 0.25 mile north of where Michigan Bluff Road dead ends at the pack horse trail. This steep dirt road can be negotiated in a sedan in good weather. Follow this road 4 miles and several thousand feet down the northern face of the bluff overlooking the Middle Fork of the American River until it joins the Mosquito Ridge Road near the North Fork of the Middle Fork of the American River.

As you ascend from the crossing of the North Fork of the Middle Fork of the American River you will have an excellent view of the Deadwood Divide at 3 miles where the road turns sharply right. At 10 miles

DEADWOOD

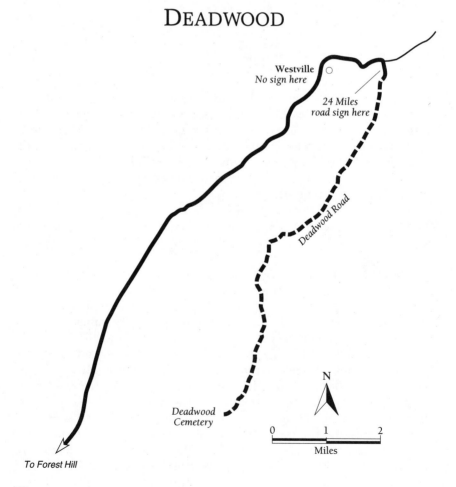

Westville
No sign here

*24 Miles
road sign here*

Deadwood Road

N

Deadwood
Cemetery

0   1   2
Miles

To Forest Hill

DUTCH FLAT

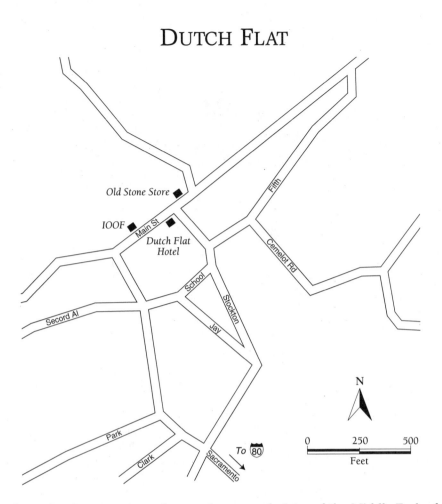

from the river crossing, after passing several vistas of the Middle Fork of the American River, take the Big Oak Flat Road to the left. This road leads only a few hundred yards but takes you into a grove of huge oak trees. This area is reportedly where Marshall spent some time prospecting in 1850.

Four miles farther is the Big Trees Grove, a beautiful, deep woods setting for a small grove of sierra redwoods.

Return to Foresthill.

Depending on your schedule and desire to explore more of this spectacular high country, a drive from Foresthill to Colfax on I-80 via Yankee Jim's Road will allow you to experience another twenty miles of hills and canyons along Shirt Tail Creek Canyon. This drive, on a mostly dirt road, takes about 1 hour, depending on the condition of the road. An even more ambitious return route with more spectacular scenery is by way of Iowa Hill. Inquire in Foresthill before taking either route.

For a quick return to CA-49, take Foresthill Road to Auburn.

Old Stone Store—a.k.a. Dutch Flat Trading Post.

DUTCH FLAT

Dutch Flat, founded in 1851, east of Auburn about 25 miles, is one of the more picturesque of the small mountain towns in the Northern Mines. Its wooden buildings add a quaint charm to this town which is just off I-80. The I.O.O.F. building (1858) is still used for local social functions. The massive 2-story Dutch Flat Hotel (1852) stands empty and fenced off. Although its future seems uncertain, townspeople open the hotel for special occasions. The Old Stone Store (1854), across Main Street from the hotel, is still in use.

After completing your tour of the various areas of Placer County, return to CA 49 and proceed north to Grass Valley in Nevada County.

PLACER COUNTY TRAVEL INFORMATION

PLACER COUNTY VISITOR INFORMATION AND FILM OFFICE
Telephone: 800-427-6463 or 916-887-2111; FAX 916-887-2134
Mailing and Street Address: 13464 Lincoln Way, Auburn, CA 95603

Jimtown 1849 Gold Mining Camp in Jamestown recreates life in a gold rush era camp.

The Fricot nugget (inset) is displayed at the California State Mining and Mineral Museum in Mariposa.

The Sutter's Mill Replica at Coloma stands near the site of the original built by James W. Marshall.

The Plumas-Eureka State Park preserves the gold mining operation that began in 1851 and continued until 1943.

Bodie is the best known "ghost town" in California's Gold Rush Country.

Railtown 1897's Sierra Railway has been the setting for many western films, including Back To The Future III *and the television series,* Petticoat Junction.

This placid setting on the Carson River is on Highway 88 near Carson Pass.

Visitors learn how to pan for gold at Matelot Gulch in Columbia State Historic Park.

*The Knight's Ferry Covered Bridge, built in 1864,
was on the important supply road from Stockton to Sonora.*

*The historic Jackson Gate House, at Jackson, is one
of many "bed and breakfasts" that provide comfortable accommodations in California's Gold Rush
Country.*

*The Kentucky Mine at Sierra City offers a glimpse
into hard rock mining with exhibits and tours.*

*Gold is still found
at Rich Bar in
Plumas County.*

These rocks were uncovered by miners in their search for gold at Columbia.

Docents recreate an arrest at the Columbia Jail in Columbia State Historic Park.

Stagecoach rides are very popular at Columbia State Historic Park.

The State Capitol in Sacramento.

Chapter   Thirteen

NEVADA COUNTY

Nevada County is the most urbanized and populated area (almost 100,000 residents) in California's Gold Rush Country. Even so, there are rugged and remote areas. The county extends from the low foothills, across the Sierra Nevada to the Nevada–California state line. There are a number of excellent museums in Nevada County to explain the history of the Gold Rush and the area.

While CA 49 has 4 lanes at the southern entrance from Placer County, there are no traffic lights on the highway in Nevada County. Both Grass Valley and Nevada City have a number of motels, bed & breakfasts, RV facilities, and restaurants, which make the area a natural overnight stop.

The story that "the streets of California are paved with gold" likely got its start in 1874 in Nevada County. When the city fathers of Grass Valley decided to pave its Main Street, they used tailings (often times laden with specks and and small nuggets of gold) from the nearby Empire Mine for foundation before sealing with pavement. Just about every man in town sifted through the tailings looking for flakes and nuggets before the street was sealed.

Visitors to Nevada County can easily spend a day in Grass Valley and Nevada City visiting museums and other local attractions. Side trips are a must to experience several historic sites that are unique to Nevada County. They are Rough and Ready, the site of a failed effort to secede from the union, Bridgeport, site of the longest single-span covered bridge west of New York State, and French Corral, site of the world's first long-distance telephone line, and Malakoff Diggins State Historic Park.

GRASS VALLEY OVERVIEW

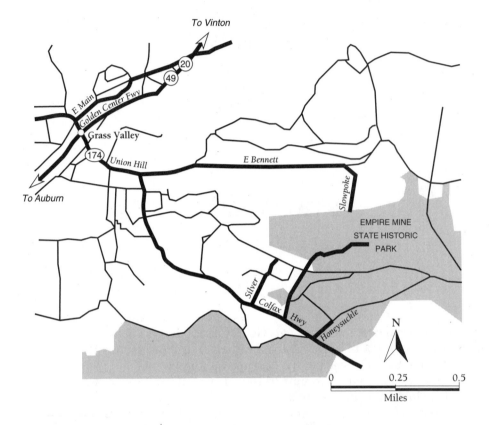

To Vinton

Grass Valley

E Main

Golden Center Fwy

Union Hill

E Bennett

To Auburn

Slowpoke

EMPIRE MINE
STATE HISTORIC
PARK

Silver

Colfax Hwy

Honeysuckle

N

0   0.25   0.5

Miles

Malakoff Diggins is 1 of 4 spectacular "diggins" in California's Gold Rush Country which were created by giant monitors, high pressure nozzles, that sprayed huge geysers of water onto the surrounding mountains literally washing them away. Malakoff Diggins is marked by devastated land, eerily carved into miniature replicas of the Grand Canyon.

For those with the time, a side trip to Washington and Truckee will complete the Nevada County experience.

TOURING GRASS VALLEY

Settled by gold miners from Boston in 1849, this grassy valley was first known as Boston Ravine. Pioneers passing through on the Truckee Pass Emigrant Trail found an abundance of green grass suitable for forage for their livestock.

Grass Valley has a well preserved downtown with a number of historic buildings. Foremost among them is the Holbrooke Hotel (1861), which has welcomed United States' Presidents Ulysses Grant, Benjamin

GRASS VALLEY

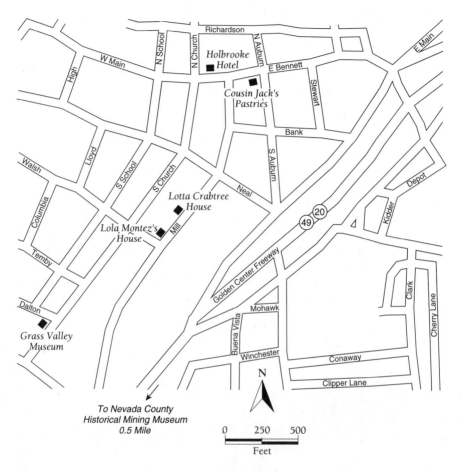

Harrison, Grover Cleveland, and James Garfield. Other notable guests include Mark Twain, Bret Harte, and Grass Valley celebrity Lotta Crabtree. The Holbrooke Hotel incorporated the Golden Gate Saloon (1852), which has a magnificent bar that was shipped around Cape Horn. The Golden Gate Saloon is the oldest continuously operating saloon in California's Gold Rush Country. The Holbrooke Hotel, 212 Main Street, Grass Valley 95945; 916-273-1353 or 800-933-7077; FAX: 916-273-0434.

Two of Grass Valley's most famous residents, Lola Montez and Lotta Crabtree, were well known dancers in the Gold Rush mining camps. Montez, also known as Countess of Landsfeld, is best remembered for her erotic Spider Dance, which created quite a stir in Gold Rush dance halls. She built a cabin (circa 1852) at present day 248 Mill Street where she lived with her pet bear. Her cabin, much renovated, now serves as the headquarters of the Nevada County Convention and Visitor Bureau and the Grass Valley and Nevada County Chamber of Commerce.

Lotta Crabtree, who lived 3 doors away at 238 Mill Street (circa 1853), became a young protégé of Lola Montez. Lotta had a successful dance career and lived in San Francisco until her death at age 77.

Downtown Grass Valley retains much of the charm of its past. By 1890, Grass Valley was populated heavily by miners and families from Cornwall, England. The pasty, a tasty meat pie dish favored by the Cornish miners who worked in the mines of the area, is still popular here. You can try a pasty at Cousin Jack Pasties at the corner of South Auburn and Main Street in Grass Valley.

The Cornish Christmas Celebration is a yearly Christmas season feature held in downtown Grass Valley to commemorate the heritage of its pioneer settlers.

Quartz (hard-rock) mining had its origins in Grass Valley at the Gold Hill Mine in 1852. Other famous quartz mines in the area include the Eureka and the North Star. The Empire Mine, now known as the Empire Mine State Historic Park, combined with the North Star Mine to form one of the largest gold mines in the world. More than 5.8 million ounces of gold were extracted between 1850 and 1956.

The main shaft extended 4,600 feet on an incline with a lower level that reached to the 8,000-foot level on an incline. When combined with the North Star, the Empire reached to a depth of 11,007 feet on an incline of about 1 vertical mile below the surface. There are more than 367 miles of tunnels below the surface of the area.

Empire Mine State Historic Park.

The world's largest Pelton Wheel is on display at the Nevada County Historical Mining Museum.

The Bourn Cottage, home to the Manager of the Empire Mine, has carefully groomed grounds with colorful gardens on display each spring. Surrounding the Bourn Cottage is 1 of just 2 formal gardens that remain from the Gold Rush in California's Gold Rush Country. (The other is in Sank Park in Oroville). The Empire Mine State Historic Park, 10791 East Empire Street, Grass Valley, CA 95945; 916-273-8522. Fee.

The Grass Valley Museum (1865), housed in a former Gold Rush era orphanage, has excellent period displays of everyday life in the area. The Grass Valley Museum, 410 South Church Street, Grass Valley, CA 95945. 916-272-4725. Seasonal. Donation. The North Star Mine, now known as the Nevada County Historical Mining Museum, displays the world's largest Pelton Wheel. Built in 1896, the wheel is 30 feet in diameter. Powered by water, Pelton Wheels like the 1 on display here was used to operate equipment throughout the Northern Mines. The Nevada County Historical Mining Museum is located at the end of Mill Street at Allison Ranch Road, Grass Valley; 916-273-4235. The museum is open from May 1 through Labor Day. The Pelton Wheel's inventor, Lester Allen Pelton, lived in nearby Camptonville. (See Yuba County, page 166). Grass Valley has a number of Victorian homes that add to the charm of its residential areas. The hillsides are especially lovely in the spring when fruit trees bloom and colorful in the fall when the maples imported by the 49ers turn shades of gold, red and oranges. Among the many Victorian homes built in Grass Valley in the late 1800s, the Tremoureux House, at 403 Neal Street, is especially attractive during fall foliage season. The huge maple in its front yard was planted here in 1876. The tree was dug up as a sapling from the Civil War Battlefield at Gettysburg and brought around Cape Horn by ship.

Nevada City is just 2 miles north of Grass Valley. The view from CA 49 as you approach the town is impressive. Nevada City is surrounded by hills that create a pleasant panorama.

Exit CA 49 at Broad Street. Turn left at the end of the exit ramp and cross over CA 49 to enter the historic district of Nevada City.

TOURING NEVADA CITY

The largest collection of extant Gold Rush buildings in California's Gold Rush Country stands within the downtown area of Nevada City. Most of these buildings are along Broad Street, lower Commercial Street and lower Main Street. From The National Hotel to the Methodist Church at the top of Nabob Hill, a distance of 0.5 mile, Broad Street is lined with Gold Rush-era buildings that create a historic ambiance unlike any other in California's Gold Rush Country. Although a fire destroyed most of Nevada City's central district in November 1863, much of this area remains as was rebuilt in 1864.

James W. Marshall is reported to have prospected in midsummer 1848 in Deer Creek, which courses through central Nevada City.

NEVADA CITY

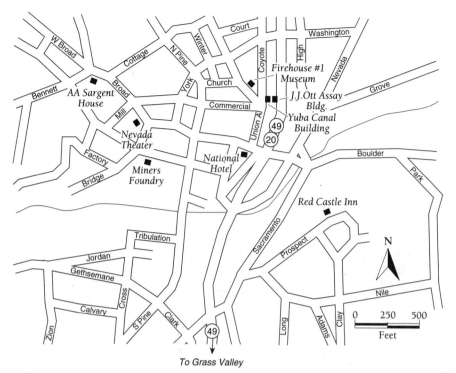

To Grass Valley

Highlights to see in Nevada City include the Firehouse #1 Museum (1861) at the intersections of Union, Commercial, and Main Streets. This museum operated by the Nevada County Historical Society contains excellent displays including an altar from a Chinese Joss House, Maidu Indian artifacts, and relics from the Donner Party which met its fate in the Sierra Nevada near present day Truckee. Firehouse #1 Museum, 214 Main Street, Nevada City, CA 95959; 916-265-5468. Firehouse #2 (1861), stands at the "top of Broad Street" on Nabob Hill, and continues to serve Nevada City as a fire station. Another notable museum is the Searls Historical Library (1872), rich in historical pictures and books pertinent to early county history. The Searls Historical Library, 214 Church Street, Nevada City; 916-265-5910. Seasonal. Donations.

The Nevada Theater (1865) is home to the Foothill Theatre Company, the oldest repertory group in California's Gold Rush Country. The Nevada Theater, 402 Broad Street, 916-265-8587. The J.J. Ott Assay Office (1857 and 1863) is where the first samples of silver ore from the Washoe Lake area in Nevada were tested. This discovery of the Comstock Lode led to the great silver rush in Nevada City, Nevada, in 1859 and heralded the end of the California Gold Rush.

The J. J. Ott Assay Office (right).

The Yuba Canal Building (1855), which served as headquarters to California's largest canal system, is adjacent to the J.J. Ott Assay Office. Today, the Yuba Canal Building serves as headquarters for the Nevada City Chamber of Commerce, 132 Main Street, Nevada City 95959; 916-265-2692. In front of these 2 buildings is a Pelton Wheel, which was used in the nearby Drum Powerhouse on the Bear River by Pacific Gas & Electric before being placed on display here in the mid 1980s.

The National Hotel.

The Miners Foundry Cultural Center (1856) at 325 Spring Street is where Lester Pelton invented the first of his Pelton Wheels in 1878; 916-265-5040.

The Kidd-Knox Building (1856) stands at the intersection of Broad Street and Pine Street. Lola Montez is reported to have performed her famous "Spider Dance" in the Kidd-Knox Building. According to Ed Tyson, Nevada County historian, Lola most likely performed in a dance hall in the Hamlet-Davis Building, which preceded the current building.

The National Hotel, built between 1854 and 1857, stands as the finest of the Gold Rush-era hotels remaining in California's Gold Rush Country. The National Hotel is the oldest, continuously operating hotel west of the Mississippi River. Its guests have included Herbert Hoover, Lola Montez, Black Bart and Lotta Crabtree. The Pacific Gas and Electric Company was organized here in 1898. The magnificent square grand piano in the hotel lobby and the bar in the lounge were shipped around Cape Horn.

Horse drawn carriage service is available seasonally in Nevada City to help recreate a Gold Rush atmosphere when horses provided the power for travelers. Take a ride around town for a fresh perspective on the old fashioned way to see the sights.

A number of residences from the early days remain to provide travelers with a glimpse of the simplicity and the elegance of the Gold Rush. Most notable among these are the A. A. Sargent House (1856) and the Red Castle Inn (1860).

This square piano was shipped around Cape Horn.

Main Street, Nevada City.

The A. A. Sargent House, a prominent 3-story Colonial Revival on Nabob Hill at 449 Broad Street, is operated as Grandmêre's Bed and Breakfast. Sargent, a 49er from Massachusetts, was important to the early development of Nevada City and California. He became the editor and publisher of Nevada City's first newspaper, the Nevada Journal (1851). Politically active, he served 2 terms in the US Congress and one term as a Senator. He championed woman's suffrage and authored the Anthony Amendment which eventually was voted into law in 1918 without change to what he had written some 40 years earlier: "The right of citizens of the United States to vote shall not be denied or abridged by the United States or any state on account of sex." Ellen Clark Sargent was one of the early suffragists in the United States and the first in Nevada County. Susan B. Anthony was a frequent guest in the house. Today, 7 rooms are available for overnight guests. Grandmêre's, 449 Broad Street, Nevada City, CA 95959; 916-265-4660.

Equally prominent on Prospect Hill is the multi-gabled Red Castle Inn at 109 Prospect Street. From the verandah and several balconies, one can look down upon Nevada City from this spectacular 4-story brick building. The view is particularly colorful in the fall when autumn leaves turn colors all over Nevada City. Quiet elegance is an understatement in the main sitting room. The Red Castle Inn, 109 Prospect Street, Nevada City, CA 95959; 916-265-5135.

A yearly feature during the Christmas Season is the Victorian Christmas celebrated in downtown Nevada City. Fall foliage tours are popular here in October.

145

Once you have completed your tour of Nevada City, several options exist. Before you move north toward Yuba and Sierra Counties on CA 49, a side trip to Rough and Ready, Bridgeport, and French Corral is well worth consideration. This diversion through scenic countryside takes about 1 hour and puts you farther north on CA 49.

Return to Grass Valley on CA 49 South. Exit at East Main Street and proceed west past The Holbrooke Hotel. West Main Street becomes the Rough and Ready Highway. At 4 miles from downtown Grass Valley, enter the village of Rough and Ready.

TOURING ROUGH AND READY, BRIDGEPORT AND FRENCH CORRAL

Rough and Ready is distinguished as the only town to secede from the Union in California's Gold Rush Country. On April 7, 1850, prior to California becoming a state, in a moment of pique at a government-imposed miners tax and a general mood of opposition to the government,

ROUGH AND READY SIDE TRIP

Bridgeport Covered Bridge.

the 3,000 townspeople voted to secede from the Union. They elected a President, signed a constitution and formed a new state, the State of Rough and Ready. The secession was short lived when the actions taken were largely ignored. However, commemorations are held each June 30 to recall the tiny town's brief moment of statehood.

The first building on the right, on the north side of the Rough and Ready Highway, is the Fippin Blacksmith Shop (circa 1850s). Lotta Crabtree reportedly danced on the anvil of the Fippin Blacksmith Shop when she was 6 years old. One hundred yards farther west is a small park area. Up the hill at 100 yards is the I.O.O.F. building (1850s) which serves as the community hall for Rough and Ready.

Continue west on the Rough and Ready Highway for 1 mile to CA 20. Turn right and go west for 3 miles to Pleasant Valley Road. Turn right and travel 8 miles to Bitney Springs Road. Proceed straight ahead for 3 miles to the South Fork of the Yuba River and the Bridgeport Covered Bridge.

The Bridgeport Covered Bridge is distinguished as being the longest single span covered west of New York State with a free clearance of 209 feet. This was, and remains, an impressive feat for nineteenth technology.

The Bridgeport Covered Bridge, built in 1862 by David I. Wood of lumber milled at Forest City in nearby Sierra County, has been bypassed in favor of a modern concrete bridge. The old bridge was built as part of the toll road that ran from Marysville to Virginia City, Nevada, by way of

Henness Pass. Despite the age of the bridge, its massive wooden beams are still structurally sound. A small park, offering picnic facilities, is operated by the California Department of Parks and Recreation as the South Yuba River Project. Trails lead along the South Fork of the Yuba River for those who wish to hike. South Yuba River Project, 17660 Pleasant Valley Road, Penn Valley, CA 95946; 916-432-2546.

Continue north on Pleasant Valley Road up the steep grade for 3 miles to French Corral. The only building that remains here of this once extremely important and active community is a sturdy Wells Fargo Building (1853). One mile farther on the right side of the road is the remnant of the French Corral Diggins.

No area in California's Gold Rush Country had more hydraulic mining activity than that of northern Nevada County along the San Juan Ridge. This area, on the ancient San Juan River channel, contained, and by some estimates still harbors, hundreds of millions of dollars in gold nuggets. Beginning in the early 1850s, with the development of hydraulic mining, a number of water companies created a series of lakes in the high Sierras in the eastern end of Nevada County and linked these lakes with canals leading along the San Juan Ridge to French Corral at the western end of the county.

This intricate system of canals and ditches ran from Bowman Lake to Graniteville, Malakoff Diggins, North Bloomfield, and North San Juan, and ended at French Corral. Water from these canals was used to operate

Malakoff Diggins.

MALAKOFF DIGGINS

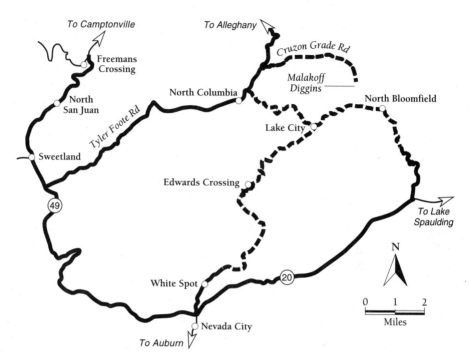

To Camptonville

To Alleghany

Cruzon Grade Rd

Freemans
Crossing

Malakoff
Diggins

North Columbia

North Bloomfield

North
San Juan

Tyler Foote Rd

Lake City

Sweetland

Edwards Crossing

49

To Lake
Spaulding

N

White Spot

20

0   1   2
Miles

Nevada City

To Auburn

the huge nozzles, called monitors, which washed away hills and mountains so that the miners could get to gold-rich gravel buried below.

The use of hydraulic mining continued until the 1884 Sawyer Decision, at which time almost all such activity terminated. By this time,
most of the creeks and rivers had been clogged with debris washed down
from the many "diggins" and agricultural interests in the valleys below
had been harmed. The French Corral Diggins stand as a colorful, silent
sentinel to a bygone era.

French Corral was the home of the Milton Mining and Water Company and the terminus of the world's first long-distance telephone line
built in 1878. More than 60 miles in length, the long-distance line was
built in cooperation with other water companies. The telephone line provided communication to help maintain the network of ditches and canals
from French Corral to Bowman Lake.

Proceed 5 miles to CA 49. To continue north on CA 49 to Sierra
County, turn left.

To visit Malakoff Diggins State Historic Park, turn right on CA 49
and drive 2 miles to Tyler Foote Road. Drive 12 miles east on Tyler Foote
Road until the roads splits with Alleghany to the left. Go right on Cruzon
Grade Road for 8 miles. Turn right and go down the hill to the entrance
to Malakoff Diggins State Historic Park.

TOURING MALAKOFF DIGGINS

A visit to Malakoff Diggins State Historic Park is necessary to truly understand the impact that the 49ers made on the landscape of California's Gold Rush Country. Here, thousands of acres of mountain sides were washed away by hydraulic mining using giant nozzles.

Malakoff Diggins was the largest of the numerous Nevada County "diggins." Between 1851 and 1884, when mining activity was stopped as a result of the Sawyer Decision, about $3.5 million in gold was taken from the sluice boxes. Now known as Malakoff Diggins State Historic Park, the site covers more than 3,000 acres.

Numerous wooden dams were built in the high Sierra Nevada to supply water for hydraulic mining. The water to operate the monitors at Malakoff Diggins came from Bowman Lake through the North Bloomfield ditch operated by the North Bloomfield Gravel Mining Company. More than 100 years later, the Malakoff Diggins serve as a stark reminder of the drastic efforts made by miners to dig away hillsides in their frantic search for gold.

The Kings Saloon and the Drug Store at North Bloomfield are reconstructions of older buildings dating to the 1860s and 1870s. The E Clampus Vitus is helping to restore the Carter House (1851) which originally served as a hotel. An excellent museum is located at the park headquarters.

Dramatic views of the vast areas devastated by the hydraulic mining can be seen from 0.5 miles to 3 miles away from the museum.

North San Juan.

Malakoff Diggins State Historic Park is open year-round. Visitors who plan to visit in the winter should call ahead to determine if the road and the park are accessible. Malakoff Diggins State Historic Park, 23579 North Bloomfield Road, Nevada City, CA 95959; 916-265-2740. Fee.

Return to CA 49 when you complete your tour. If you are ending your tour of California's Gold Rush Country here, turn left and go south on CA 49. If you are continuing north, turn right and proceed 5 miles to North San Juan Hill. A few brick buildings are all that remain of historic North San Juan.

From North San Juan, CA 49 begins a winding drop down to the Middle Fork of the Yuba River and crosses Yuba County. The next 49 miles, from the Yuba River to the peak of Yuba Pass in Sierra County, pass though the most scenic stretch of CA 49. Please see Yuba County, Page 166, for the continuation of this segment of CA 49.

TOURING WASHINGTON AND TRUCKEE

A few buildings remain to commemorate Washington's Gold Rush origin in 1849 on the banks of the Yuba River. The Washington Hotel (1856) and the rustic Trading Post Cafe (1849) are the oldest buildings that remain from a once thriving community. Rooms and food are available at the Washington Hotel. Call (916) 265-4364. Washington can be reached by taking CA 20 for 13 miles east of Grass Valley. Turn north on Washington Road for drive 6 miles.

Truckee is best known as a railroad town and the gateway to the Lake Tahoe area. The Donner Memorial State Park preserves the site where the Donner Party camped during the winter of 1846-1847 and the Emigrant Trail Museum, located in the park, provides a glimpse of the tragedy experienced by those trapped in the snow. Emigrant Trail Museum, 12593 Donner Pass Road, Truckee, CA 96161; 916-582-7892; FAX 916-582-7893. Hours: 10 A.M. to 5 P.M., Memorial Day through Labor Day; 10 A.M. to 4 P.M., Labor Day through Memorial Day. Fee.

NEVADA COUNTY TRAVEL INFORMATION

NEVADA COUNTY CONVENTION AND VISITORS BUREAU
Telephone: 800-655-4667 or 916-273-4667; FAX 916-272-5440
Mailing and Street Address: 248 Mill Street, Grass Valley, CA 95945

Chapter   Fourteen

SIERRA COUNTY

Sierra County presented a number of challenges to the 49ers. Because of steep canyon walls surrounding its rivers, access was very difficult. Winter snows came early to its rivers and passes, forcing the miners to abandon their lucrative mining activity.

Today's visitors find a number of paved roads providing access to Sierra County's rugged mountains, canyons, and rivers. Sierra County is one of the least settled counties with only a few towns set in the midst of its spectacular scenery. Loyalton, located in the lightly populated Sierra Valley, is the county's only incorporated town. Even though Sierra County is rich in Gold Rush legacy, only a few towns and communities have historic structures from that era.

Sierra County's primary tourist draw is the near-pristine beauty of its rivers, lakes, and mountains. Outdoor activities include camping, fly and bait fishing, rock climbing, boating, hunting, and the winter sports of snowmobiling and cross country skiing. Its Lakes Basin area, north of Sierra City, provides excellent fishing for sportsmen.

Tourist brochures for Sierra County compare the eastern area, the Sierra Valley, to the "wide open spaces" of the western plains of the United States and the western area to the Alps in Europe. There are significant similarities and Sierra County is a virtually year-round scenic paradise by the author's account as well.

The drive through Sierra County on CA 49, from near Camptonville to the peak of Yuba Pass, is the most scenic of the highway's 320 miles. CA 49 follows the North Fork of the Yuba River for much of the distance to its source at Yuba Pass. In the spring, dogwood tree blossoms color the

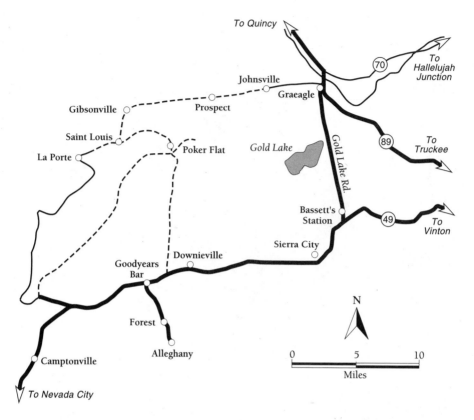

riverbanks and hill sides with their white flowers. The Yuba River flows quickly over and around huge boulders and the banks often overflow from the spring snowmelt. White water rafting and kayaking are at their peak at this time. With the snowmelt complete in late summer, fall foliage reflects serenely in small pools. This drive is spectacular in any season.

Goodyear's Bar is only 15 miles from the Yuba County-Sierra County border through the Canyon of the North Fork of the Yuba River. The river is adjacent to the highway for most of this distance.

TOURING GOODYEAR'S BAR

Goodyear's Bar, a wild mining camp in the early 1850s, at the confluence of Goodyear's Creek and the North Fork of the Yuba River, now consists of a few houses. As quiet as is today, one reminder of its past stands just 0.5 mile from CA 49, to the south, on Mountain House Road. The venerable St. Charles Hotel, built in 1864 as a stagecoach stop on the Nevada City to Downieville Road, now serves as a comfortable

153

The St. Charles Hotel was built in 1864 as a stagecoach inn.

DOWNIEVILLE

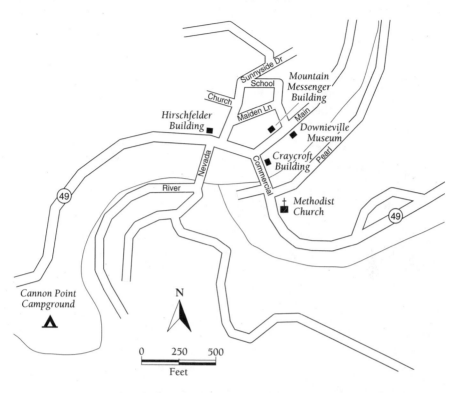

Bed & Breakfast Inn. Bullet holes decorate the ceiling of the dining room and its walls tilt because someone forgot to shovel the snow from the roof many years ago. Its 4 sleeping rooms are comfortable. The rushing Yuba River, less than 100 feet away, will quickly lull the tired traveler to sleep. Helm's St. Charles Inn, P.O. Box 49, Goodyear's Bar, CA 95944; 916-289-0910.

Beyond the St. Charles Inn, on Mountain House Road, are the remote mining camps of Forest City and Alleghany. See Side Trip to Forest City and Alleghany, page 160.

Continue north on CA 49 for 3.5 miles. At a sharp turn to the left, turn to the right into a marked parking area for an overview of Downieville.

TOURING DOWNIEVILLE

Settled in 1851, Downieville is among the prettiest towns in California's Gold Rush Country. The town is nestled in a forested canyon at the confluence of the Downie River and the North Fork of the Yuba River. Named for William Downie, who came here in November 1849 to prospect, the area quickly proved to be rich in gold. Downieville was spared the devastating fires that destroyed entire districts of early Gold Rush towns. There are 5 buildings dating from 1852 in the downtown which gives Downieville a Gold Rush era appearance. Downieville is distinguished as the site of the only hanging of a woman in all of California's Gold Rush Country.

Parking is limited in central Downieville, so use either of the 2 public parking areas provided. The first is on the right, adjacent to the River Park, and the second is at the Bell Tower (1896). Total walking distance in central Downieville, round-trip, is about 0.5 mile.

The Hirschfeldter Building (1852), first building on the left on CA 49 and across from the first public parking lot, is now used as a grocery store. Straight ahead at the intersection of CA 49 and Main Street is the Craycroft Building (1852) which served first as the Craycroft Saloon. The saloon's 70-foot bar was the longest ever in California's Gold Rush Country. Juanita, a Mexican woman who stabbed to death a miner who attacked her, fled here for protection in 1852. Despite her protests that she acted only in self defense, a "jury" quickly found her guilty and led her to the gallows. Reportedly, Juanita placed the noose around her neck, calmly addressed her "jury" with a brief farewell, and then leaped to her death. Juanita's death by hanging has remained one of the dark moments in the history of California's Gold Rush Country.

CA 49 turns right and crosses over the Downie River. On the left is the Methodist Church (1852), which is the oldest Protestant church in continuous use in California. Return to Main Street and turn right. Across the street is The Mountain Messenger Building (1852),

The North Fork of the Yuba River runs through Downieville.

Downieville Museum.

California's oldest weekly newspaper since 1853. Newspaper copies are available throughout the Northern Mines.

Almost directly across from The Mountain Messenger is the Downieville and Sierra County Museum (1852) at 330 Main Street. This old building originally served as a Chinese store and gambling house. The museum houses artifacts from Sierra County's rich Gold Rush period. Open from Memorial Day through the first weekend of October. Donations; 916-289-3423.

TOURING SIERRA CITY

The dominant feature at Sierra City is the Sierra Buttes which tower to 8,587 feet. Numerous mines were cut into these massive rocks. The second largest gold nugget discovered in California's Gold Rush Country, weighing 141 pounds, was taken from the Monumental Quartz Mine in 1869.

Founded in 1850, Sierra City was originally located high up on the steep slopes of the Sierra Buttes. Avalanches in the winter of 1852 - 1853 destroyed the town, forcing its relocation to its present location, at 4,187 feet, on the north bank of the North Fork of the Yuba River.

The Busch Building (1871); 916-862-1501 and The Sierra Buttes Inn (1873); 916-862-1300 both operate as Bed & Breakfast Inns. The Busch Building served as a Wells, Fargo & Company office. Central Sierra City is less than 2 blocks in length which makes it easy to walk everywhere in town. The Busch & Heringlake Country Inn, Main Street, P.O. Box 68, Sierra City, CA 96125;916-862-1501. The Sierra Buttes Inn, 212 Main Street, P.O. Box 320, Sierra City, CA 96125; 916-862-1300.

The Kentucky Mine Museum, operated by the Sierra County Historical Society, 1 mile east of Sierra City on CA 49, has excellent displays which depict the operation of a 10-stamp quartz mill. The Kentucky Mine originated from the Kentucky Consolidated Gold Mining Company founded in 1853. The setting, with the majestic Sierra Buttes as a backdrop, is scenic in all seasons. Kentucky Mine Museum, P.O. Box 260, Sierra City 96125; 916-862-1310. Hours: 10 A.M. to 5 P.M. Wednesday through Sunday, Memorial Day through September; weekends only in October. Fee for entry to Museum; additional fee for the tour of the Kentucky Mine Stamp Mill display.

TOURING THE LAKES BASIN VIA GOLD LAKE ROAD

The Gold Lake Road, which connects CA 49 at Bassett's Station (a stage stop established in 1863 and a great place to check your fuel gauge), with CA 70 / CA 89 at Graeagle in Plumas County, is a picturesque route. From early spring, when the snow melts until late fall, the 20 mile drive through the Lakes Basin is filled with scenic panoramas equaled by few areas in California's Gold Rush Country. There are 50 lakes in this area.

Highlights of this drive include Sand Pond (manmade from tailings of the Young America Mine), with excellent reflections of the Sierra Buttes in early morning, and numerous natural lakes including Sardine Lake (the road is restricted to four-wheel-drive vehicles only) and famous Gold Lake.

Gold Lake, the largest and northernmost of the Sierra County Lakes Basin, is the namesake of the fabled "Gold Lake" that resulted in a rush of epic proportions because of one 49er named Stoddart. In the fall of 1849, Stoddart was in an emigrant party traveling along the Lassen Trail in northern Plumas County when he became lost. Along the way, he re-

Gold Lake/Sierra City

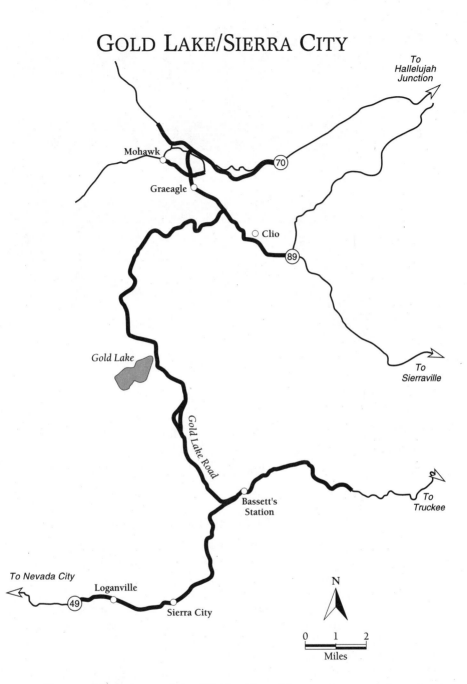

To Hallelujah Junction

Mohawk

70

Graeagle

Clio

89

To Sierraville

Gold Lake

Gold Lake Road

Bassett's Station

To Truckee

To Nevada City

Loganville

49

Sierra City

N

0   1   2
Miles

portedly stumbled upon a lake filled with gold nuggets somewhere between Downieville and Sierra Valley (in Plumas County).

When he reached safety along the North Fork of the Yuba River and related his story to other miners, it was too late in the season to go back up into the mountains. In the spring of 1850, he was joined by several

Bassett's Station.

thousand anxious miners who followed him through the lakes to the area of the Middle Fork of the Feather River in Plumas County. While he was unable to find the fabled Gold Lake, Stoddart's story is credited with opening up this region to successful mining in the gold rich rivers of Plumas County.

SIDE TRIP TO FOREST CITY AND ALLEGHANY

For those with the time and patience to negotiate a winding dirt road up to the high country, south of CA 49 on Mountain House Road from Goodyear's Bar, this side trip is an excellent opportunity to experience the scenic backcountry of the Northern Mines. Only a few houses, an old church, and a dance hall remain at Forest City to recall its importance as a gold mining camp in the early 1850s. Forest City was first founded in 1852 at the confluence of the north and south forks of Oregon Creek. Large quantities of gold were found here and a substantial town grew as the result of large scale mining activity. A major fire in 1883 destroyed much of the town. Subsequent fires in the 1930s and 1940s have all but rendered Forest City a ghost town. The town fire bell stands in a small park at the entrance to Main Street.

FOREST-ALLEGHANY

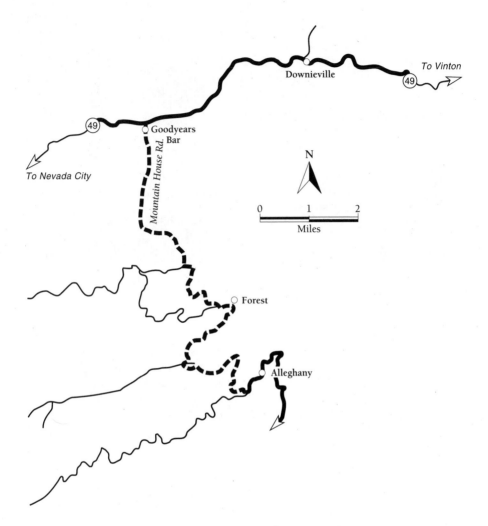

Alleghany, on Tyler Foote Road, 15 miles from Forest City, was founded as a mining camp in 1851. At a pleasant altitude of 4,300 feet, Alleghany is one of the few active mining towns in the west.

The original Sixteen to One Mine at Alleghany, on the scenic Pliocene Ridge that runs between the Middle and North Forks of the Yuba River, was established in 1896. The mine has been worked over the years with varying degrees of success. However, in 1995, a rich strike worth more than 2 million dollars was made and prospects are good for this mine to produce well into the next century.

Forest City.

I took a short guided tour through the 800-foot level in the company of Robert Olson, one of the miners. Robert showed me a number of places where major discoveries of small pockets of crystalline gold had been made. The original Sixteen to One Mine produces highly prized specimens of crystalline and "gold in quartz".

While Robert and I only viewed a small area of the mine during the hour we were underground, the original Sixteen to One Mine offers guided tours deep into its working mine through the Alleghany Mining Museum. Reservations are required and fees for underground tours range from $95 for a basic tour to the $500 Executive Tour led by the President of the mine. The Alleghany Mining Museum, 351 Main Street, provides a number of exhibits from the Original Sixteen to One Mine. Contact The Alleghany Mining Museum, P.O. Box 907, Alleghany, CA 95910; 916-287-3330; FAX 916-287-3455. Open daily from 10 A.M. to 4 P.M.

SIDE TRIP TO PORT WINE, QUEEN CITY, GIBSONVILLE, HOWLAND FLAT AND POKER FLAT

For those who can plan ahead, prepare for travel with extra food, water and camping equipment, and preferably drive a four-wheel-drive vehicle, a side trip to the remote northwest corner of Sierra County will

Robert Olson examines a quartz vein for gold at the Original Sixteen to One Mine.

be rewarded with spectacular scenery. This rugged area, which has mountain peaks in excess of 7,000 feet, includes the sites of the 1850s mining towns of Port Wine, Queen City, Gibsonville, Howland Flat, and Poker Flat.

A number of these roads, dirt and gravel, can be driven in cars during dry weather conditions. However, the road to Poker Flat is accessible only by four-wheel-drive vehicles.

Access to these areas by tourists should be limited to summer months and then only after local inquiry. This area is remote and there are no call boxes on the side of the road to summon help should you experience problems.

TOURING LOYALTON AND THE NORTHERN TERMINUS OF HIGHWAY 49

The Sierra Valley, opened to agricultural activity in the early 1850s by Swiss emigrants, became an important area for hay production. With the opening of the Yuba Gap Wagon Road in 1870, horses wearing 9-inch square "snowshoes" pulled wagons and sleds loaded with hay from the Sierra Valley to feed the horses and cattle of Sierra City and Downieville during the winter.

The Loyalton Museum, located 1 block north of CA 49 on Highway 824 (just follow the signs to the City Park from downtown), has excellent displays which feature the main industries of the area, logging and agri-

LOYALTON/VINTON

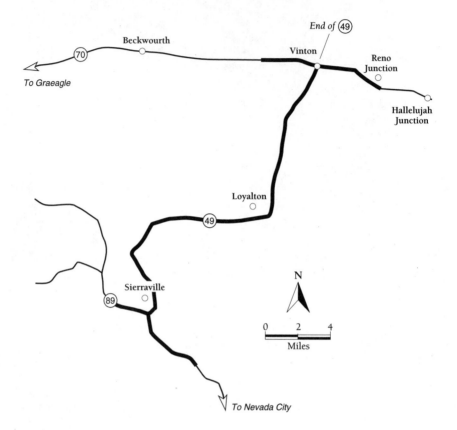

culture; 916-993-6754. Hours: 10:30 A.M. to 3:30 P.M., May through October.

To reach the end of CA 49, continue 11 miles north from Loyalton to the community of Vinton in Plumas County. With a simple sign that says, "END", CA 49 ends at CA70 in Plumas County. If you are continuing on to Plumas County, turn left (west) on CA70 and proceed toward Beckwourth and Quincy.

SIERRA COUNTY TRAVEL INFORMATION

SIERRA COUNTY VISITORS BUREAU
Telephone: 800-200-4949 or 916-993-6900; FAX 916-993-6909
Mailing Address: P.O. Box 206, Loyalton, CA 96118

Gold Lake.

Chapter Fifteen

YUBA COUNTY

Yuba County, located north of Sacramento, extends from the Sacramento River to the low foothills of the Sierra Nevada. Numerous mining camps were set up along the Yuba River but all were buried by silt from hydraulic mining upriver. Marysville, Yuba County's largest town, was rich in Gold Rush buildings. Most of these buildings were taken down in the 1960s to make way for downtown revitalization. One such building was used by Rowland H. Macy, founder of Macy's Department Stores. However, those historic buildings that remain present an impressive array of architectural styles.

Until silt from hydraulic mining far up in the Sierra Nevada clogged the Yuba, Feather, and Sacramento Rivers, Marysville was the northernmost port on the Feather River. Stagecoach roads led from Marysville to many areas of the Northern Mines. One of the most important was the Marysville–La Porte Road. Buildings used as stage stops on this road still exist at Rackerby and Woodleaf.

Yuba County is served by CA 70 from south to north and CA 20 from east to west.

TOURING CA 49 IN YUBA COUNTY

Yuba County shares a 10 mile segment of CA 49 from the Middle Fork of the Yuba River to just north of Camptonville. There are 2 highlights along CA 49. Barely 100 yards north and east of the bridge over the Middle Fork of the Yuba River, turn right on the Oregon Creek Road.

The Oregon Creek covered bridge is less than 0.2 mile ahead. Built in 1862, this bridge was washed downstream shortly after being completed. The bridge was towed back to its abutments and reinstalled reverse to its original alignment. The Oregon Creek covered bridge has served horse drawn and gasoline powered vehicles ever since.

At Camptonville, a small monument memorializes the birth here of Lester Allen Pelton, inventor of the Pelton Wheel. The Pelton Wheel proved to be perhaps the most important source of water power throughout the Northern Mines and is still in use today at some locations to generate electricity.

Continue north from Camptonville on CA 49 into Sierra County.

JOHN A. SUTTER AND WILLIAM JOHNSON

In 1842, after establishing himself at New Helvetia (Sutter's Fort), John Sutter expanded his agricultural pursuits in this area. Through land grants obtained from the Mexican Government, he controlled much of what has become Sutter and Yuba counties. He built a farm on the west side of the Feather River, about 8 miles below Marysville, which he called Hock Farm (or Upper Farm). Sutter's Hock Farm became known for its abundant orchards and fertile fields. After he lost Sutter's Fort, Sutter retired to his beloved Hock Farm. Much of the farm was covered over by silt from hydraulic mining operations during the flood of 1862. Sutter left Hock Farm in 1868 to move to Lititz, Pennsylvania.

William Johnson purchased a large block of land in 1842 on the north side of the Yuba River. Johnson, first husband of Mary Murphy of the Donner Party, settled here and built an adobe house which became well known as Johnson's Rancho to thousands of emigrants who followed the Bear River route down the Sierra Nevada to Sacramento. Numerous diaries recount the hospitality accorded by Johnson to emigrants who were in need of help after following the California Trail across the Sierra Nevada.

It was to Johnson's Rancho that the 7 members of the Forlorn Hope Party stumbled on January 7, 1847. The remaining members of the ill-fated Donner Party—including Mary Murphy—were brought here when finally rescued in February 1847. The site of Johnson's Rancho was discovered in 1985 by Jack Steed, author of *The Donner Party Rescue Site*. The site is on private property near Wheatland and is opened to the public one weekend in April of each year. Contact the Yuba–Sutter County Chamber of Commerce for the date.

The Sutter Buttes, in adjacent Sutter County (both are named in honor of John A. Sutter), are visible through much of Yuba County. Even though there are only 3 peaks, the Sutter Buttes constitute a complete mountain range.

MARYSVILLE

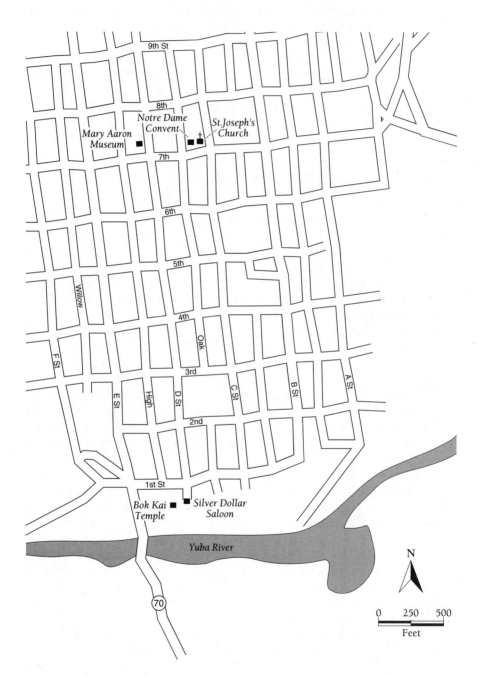

9th St

8th

Notre Dame
Convent

St.Joseph's
Church

Mary Aaron
Museum

7th

6th

5th

Willow

4th

Oak

F St

3rd

E St

High

D St

C St

B St

A St

2nd

1st St

Bok Kai
Temple

Silver Dollar
Saloon

Yuba River

70

N

0   250   500
Feet

TOURING MARYSVILLE

Marysville was built on land that was originally part of John Sutter's Ranch. On January 18, 1850, city officials were elected, making the Town of Marysville older than the State of California (September 9, 1850). Charles Covillaud, one of the founders, had Marysville named for his wife, Mary Murphy Covillaud, a survivor of the Donner Party tragedy and former wife of William Johnson. During the early years of the California Gold Rush, the Feather River was navigable to Marysville and the town prospered as a result of its proximity to the Northern Mines. Miners traveled upriver from San Francisco to Marysville before taking one of the numerous trails leading to the gold mining camps.

Marysville was the site of the first Macy's Store in California. In 1850, Rowland H. Macy left Boston—where he had been unsuccessful in several ventures—to try his luck at retailing in Marysville. He had no better luck in Marysville. He returned east and opened a small, fancy dry goods store in New York City in 1858, which proved successful.

Remaining structures of interest to visitors are primarily along "D" Street between the 700 block south to First Street. The Mary Aaron Memorial Museum is housed in a Gothic Revival house (1855). The Mary Aaron Memorial Museum, 704 "D" Street, Marysville, CA 95901; 916-743-1004. Hours: 1:30 P.M. to 4:30 P.M., Tuesday through Saturday. Nearby, on "C" Street, is the magnificent neo-Gothic structure, St. Joseph's Catholic Church (1855).

Mary Aaron Museum.

The entrance to Bok Kai Temple.

Perhaps the most interesting structures are on the north bank of the Yuba River at "D" Street and First Street. The Bok Kai Temple was first built in the early 1850s high above the Yuba River. Because sediment from hydraulic mining raised the level of the river, the current temple, built in 1880, is now behind a levee and below river level. Visitors are welcome to enter to worship or view this working temple. If you are lucky, perhaps you will visit when Soon Loy Kee, a descendant of Chinese miners, serves as a guide at the Bok Kai Temple.

The Silver Dollar Saloon (1860) was built on the site of an adobe belonging to Theodore Cordua. Cordua leased the land from Sutter and created a settlement which he called New Mecklenburg. The Silver Dollar Saloon has served as a bar, a hotel and, until 1975, a brothel.

SIDE TRIP TO SMARTVILLE AND TIMBUCTOO

For those who are traveling on CA 20 east from Marysville to Grass Valley, there are two interesting points to see while en route. At 18 miles, immediately after crossing over the Yuba River, exit onto Timbuctoo Road. This narrow, paved road leads to the site of Timbuctoo, which, as well as the next town of Smartville, was the site of extensive hydraulic mining. The site of Timbuctoo is marked by ruins of the Wells, Fargo & Company building (1855). Much of the silt and debris that raised the Yuba River by 70 feet at Marysville came from this area.

Marysville Side Trip

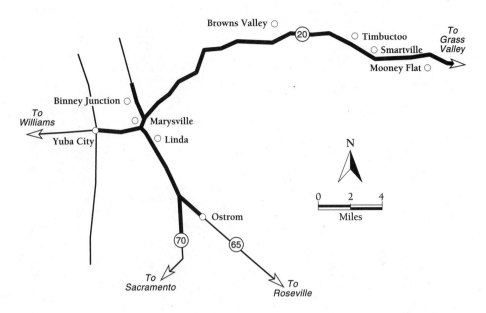

SIDE TRIP ON THE MARYSVILLE - LA PORTE ROAD VIA BROWN'S VALLEY, CHALLENGE, WOODLEAF, AND STRAWBERRY

For those who wish to follow the old Marysville–La Porte Road into the foothills and on up to La Porte in Plumas County, this is one of the more interesting drives in the area. Follow CA 20 east from Marysville for 14 miles to County Highway E21. Turn left (north), and drive 1 mile to Brown's Valley. The P&L Mercantile Building (1849) still serves as a general store to the community. Across the road, buried in blackberry vines, are the ruins of an old hotel (1852), 1 of 5 hotels built here during the 1850s.

At rackerby, the Rackerby Stage Stop (1861) has been maintained in excellent condition.

The prettiest building, however, is the lovely Woodleaf Hotel (1856) built as the Woodville House. Located in the small community of Woodleaf, the hotel served as a California Stage Company station on the Marysville–La Porte Road.

A 4 mile diversion from the Marysville–La Porte Road to Forbestown will allow you to see the well preserved I.O.O.F. building (1855) at Forbestown and an excellent country museum, the Yuba Feather Historical Museum on the New York Flat Road (ask before turning off E21 at Brownsville). The museum, located in an old schoolhouse, features exhibits of mining and logging equipment, a country store and basketry of

171

Old cabin in Strawberry Valley.

the Maidu Indians. Open weekends and holidays from Memorial Day through Labor Day; 916-675-2800.

Strawberry Valley is the last community in Yuba County. La Porte, at the end of the Marysville–La Porte Road, is another 15 miles ahead in Plumas County (See Plumas County, page 184).

YUBA AND SUTTER COUNTY TRAVEL INFORMATION

YUBA-SUTTER CHAMBER OF COMMERCE
Telephone: 916-743-6501; FAX 916-741-8645
Mailing Address: P.O. Box 1429, Marysville, CA 95901
Street Address: 429 Tenth Street

MARYSVILLE–LA PORTE

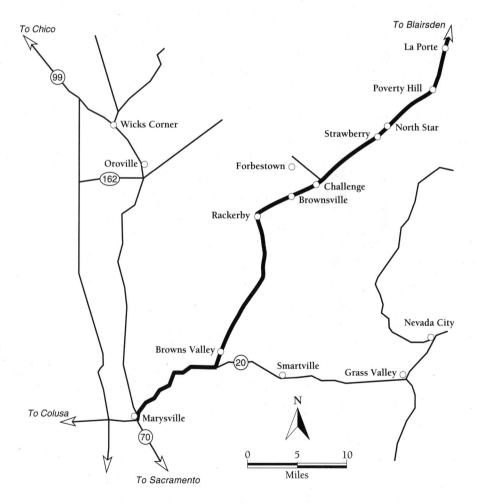

BROWNSVILLE

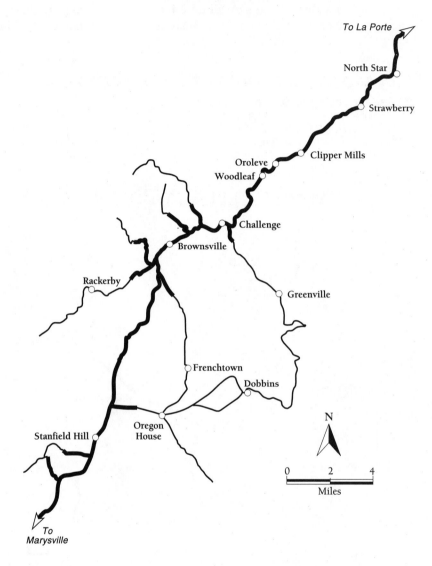

To La Porte

North Star

Strawberry

Clipper Mills

Oroleve

Woodleaf

Challenge

Brownsville

Rackerby

Greenville

Frenchtown

Dobbins

Stanfield Hill

Oregon House

N

0   2   4
Miles

To
Marysville

LA PORTE

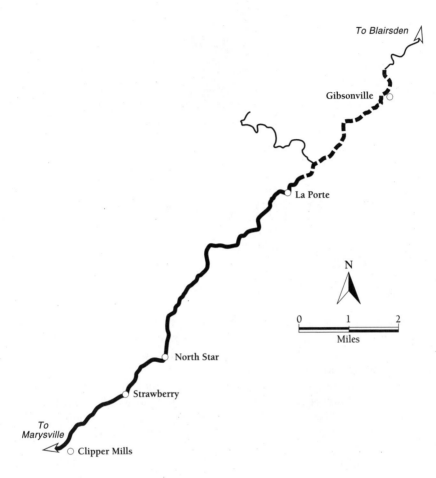

To Blairsden

Gibsonville

La Porte

N

0   1   2
Miles

North Star

Strawberry

*To
Marysville*

Clipper Mills

BUTTE COUNTY

Butte County is a lightly populated area that extends from the Sacramento River on the west to the low foothills bordering Yuba County and Plumas County. Lake Oroville provides a major source of outdoor activity for residents and tourists alike.

Oroville was, for a few years, the largest town in California's Gold Rush Country. John Bidwell discovered gold in July 1848 at what became known as Bidwell Bar on the Middle Fork of the Feather River near its confluence with the North Fork of the Feather River. Oroville became one of the most important gold mining camps on the Feather River. Much of the Feather River in this area was flumed out of its banks and the riverbed was mined for gold nuggets.

Oroville became the county seat in 1856, replacing Bidwell Bar, and served as an important regional outfitting and transportation center for the Northern Mines. More importantly, however, Oroville and nearby Cherokee became the setting for the world's largest hydraulic mining activity, which caused large scale destruction of the surrounding landscape from the late 1850s until the late 1880s.

River dredging for gold was developed at Oroville and led to farther digging up of the confluence of the North and Middle Forks of the Feather River leaving huge piles of tailings along the river banks. Dredging spread from Oroville to rivers throughout California. Large quantities of gold were taken from this gold rich area. For this reason, Oroville is also known as the "City of Gold."

Virtually all signs of these gold dredging activities have been covered over by the waters of Lake Oroville.

BUTTE COUNTY

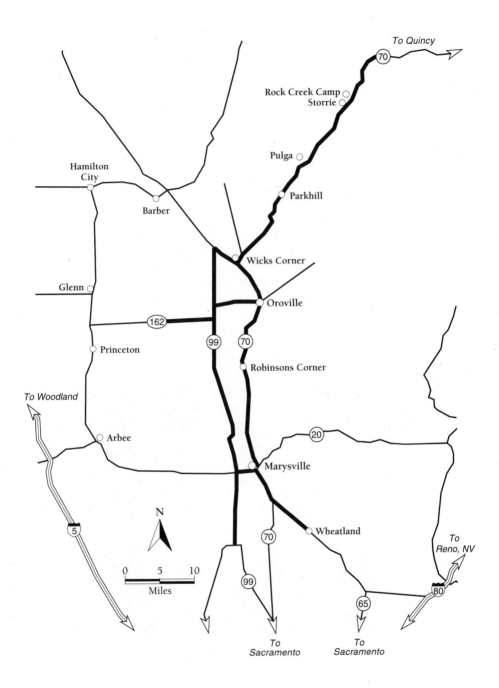

TOURING OROVILLE

Oroville, which means City of Gold, is one of the loveliest cities in the Northern Mines. In the spring, flowers color the gardens of Oroville and the fields and hillsides of Table Mountain above this town, which was first called Ophir City. In 1854 and 1855, there were some 10,000 miners in and around Oroville, making it the largest city in California's Gold Rush Country at the time.

The C. F. Lott House (1856) is a Victorian gothic revival style house. The Lott House's formal garden, 1 of only 2 dating to the Gold Rush that remain in California's Gold Rush Country, forms the setting for the lovely Sank Park. The other garden is at the Bourn Cottage on the grounds of the Empire Mine State Historic Park in Grass Valley. Sank Park, 1067 Montgomery Street, Oroville, CA 95966; 916-538-2497. Park Hours: 9 A.M. to 9 P.M., Monday through Saturday, 9 A.M. to 8:30 P.M., Sunday.

The Oroville Chinese Temple (1863) was the religious center of Oroville's community of 10,000 Chinese. The temple's 3 chapels, various exhibits and Chinese gardens, provide a glimpse into this important aspect of the Chinese miner's life. Oroville Chinese Temple, 1500 Broderick Street, Oroville, CA 95965; 916-538-2496. Hours: Thursday to Monday, 11 A.M. to 4:30 P.M., Tuesday and Wednesay, 1 P.M. to 4 P.M. Closed: December 15 through January.

This giant urn stands in front of the Oroville Chinese Temple.

OROVILLE

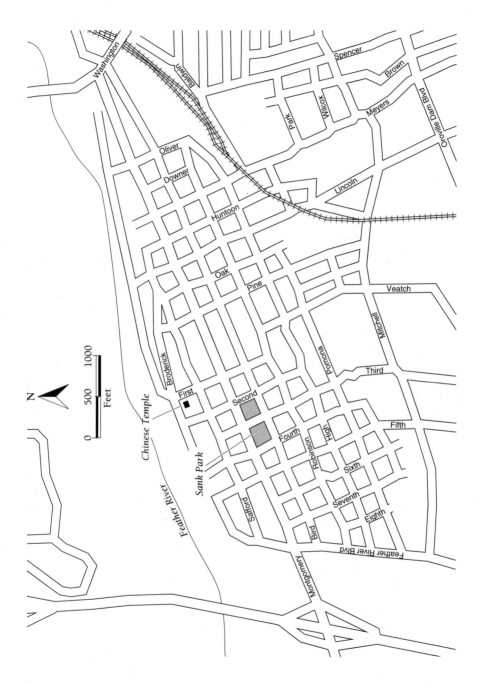

Oroville Dam, completed in 1968, is the tallest (770 feet) and largest earth dam in the United States. Oroville Lake, a project of the State Department of Water Resources, covers more than 24 square miles.

Bidwell Bar lies below the waters but several important artifacts from that site were relocated to the Bidwell Canyon area of the Lake Oroville State Recreation Area. They are the Bidwell Bar Bridge and its Toll House. The suspension bridge, manufactured on the east coast of the United States and shipped by boat around Cape Horn, was installed across the Middle Fork of the Feather River in 1856. The bridge was used until 1954 before being closed to vehicular traffic.

The Oroville area has modern motels, bed & breakfasts, RV facilities, and restaurants, making the area an ideal overnight stop whether traveling to or from the Northern Mines.

TOURING TABLE MOUNTAIN AND CHEROKEE

Rising above Oroville, and visible for many miles, Table Mountain is one of the interesting geological features of the area. Created from a lava flow, Table Mountain is carpeted with flowers in the spring and summer, creating a setting of scenic grandeur as you look to the Sacramento Valley and the Sierra Buttes to the west and to the Sierra Nevada to the east.

From central Oroville, follow Table Mountain Boulevard for 1 mile; turn right on Cherokee Road and drive 10 miles to Cherokee. For the first 2 miles, the road winds and curves along the edge of Table Mountain by the Feather River just below the spillway of Lake Oroville Dam. The road makes a steep, 2-mile climb up the side to the top of Table Mountain.

You will want to stop at one of the numerous pulloffs and take in the views in all directions.

At Oregon Gulch Road, turn right for 2 miles to the site of Oregon City. The Oregon City School (1877) is the only remnant of the once-thriving Oregon City. The school building now houses a museum. Oregon City was founded in 1848 by a group of Oregonians led by Peter Burnett who became the first civil Governor of California.

Continue on Cherokee Road for 5 miles to Cherokee. Sugar Loaf Mountain rises above the site of the Spring Valley Mine at Cherokee on the north side of Table Mountain. Years of hydraulic mining created the world's largest "diggins" where millions of dollars in gold were unearthed by the Spring Valley Hydraulic Gold Company and its predecessors. The Spring Valley Mine was the site of the first discovery of diamonds in California.

Discovered by white settlers in 1849, and named for a band of Cherokee Indians from Oklahoma who mined here, the town of Cherokee was founded in 1853. The Cherokee Diggins were so rich that claims were limited to 100 square feet. By 1876, all of the mining operations in the area merged into the Spring Valley Hydraulic Gold Company, with

Oregon Gulch School.

over 100 miles of tunnels and flumes to bring water to operate 18 monitors. The consolidation made it the world's largest hydraulic gold mine.

Cherokee boasted 17 saloons, 8 hotels, 3 schools, 3 churches, several lodges, a race track, and a brewery. To commemorate America's centennial, the world's largest gold bar was cast at Cherokee. The bar weighed 260 avoirdupois or 317 pounds troy and was valued at $76,000. Four years later, in 1880, President Rutherford B. Hayes and wife, Lucy, General W. T. Sherman, and General John Bidwell visited Cherokee. A year later, a disastrous fire destroyed much of Cherokee.

The Cherokee Mine Superintendent's house now serves as the Cherokee Museum. The house has served in prior years as a stage stop, a residence, and miners' boarding house. The remains of the Spring Valley Mine and Assay Office, which burned in a fire in 1947, are across the road from the Cherokee Museum. Numerous displays include gold mining artifacts, bottles, and photos and other memorabilia from the early days at the Cherokee Mine. Cherokee Museum, 4226 Cherokee Road, Cherokee; 916-533-1849. Open weekends from May through October.

Continue west on the Cherokee Road for 1 mile to CA70. Turn left, south, to return to Cherokee. Turn right, north, and proceed "up the hill" to the Feather River National Scenic Byway and Plumas County.

OROVILLE/TABLE MOUNTAIN/CHEROKEE

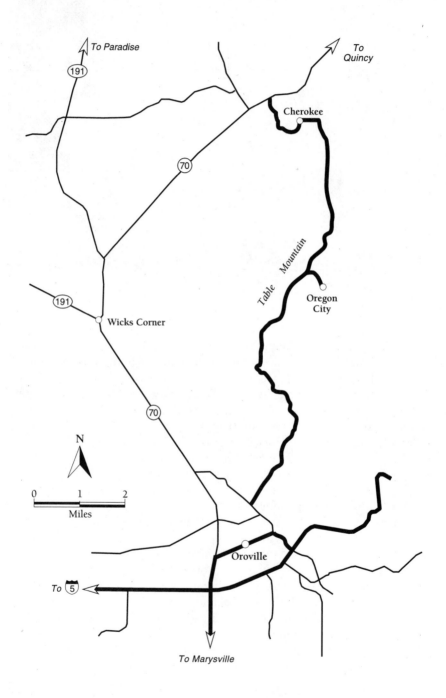

To Paradise

191

To Quincy

Cherokee

70

Table Mountain

Oregon City

191

Wicks Corner

70

N

0   1   2
Miles

Oroville

To 5

To Marysville

Artifacts at the Cherokee Museum.

SIDE TRIP TO BIDWELL STATE HISTORIC PARK

Butte County and California benefited from the services of one of the early settlers in the area, John Bidwell, later known as General John Bidwell. He was one of the co-leaders of the 1841 wagon train to California for the purpose of establishing agricultural pursuits. After working for John Sutter for several years, he bought Rancho Chico and founded the Town of Chico here in 1860. He was one of the first to participate in the California Gold Rush. His discovery of gold on the Middle Fork of the Feather River near Oroville led to the major mining operations that followed.

During his lifetime, Bidwell was active in the California militia, state and national politics, agriculture, and was one of the first to participate in the California Gold Rush. General and Mrs. Bidwell left a rich legacy of service to California. Their home has been preserved, with numerous period displays, at the Bidwell Mansion State Historic Park just off CA 99 at 525 Esplanade Street, Chico, CA 95927; 916-895-6144.

BUTTE COUNTY TRAVEL INFORMATION

OROVILLE CHAMBER OF COMMERCE
Telephone: 800-655-4654 or 916-538-2542; FAX 916-538-2546
Mailing and Street Address: 1789 Montgomery Street, Oroville, CA 95965

Chapter Seventeen

PLUMAS COUNTY

All of the superlatives used to describe the geography and scenic beauty of Sierra County apply equally to Plumas County. Both counties share the same mountain boundaries. Plumas County's primary tourist draw is the near-pristine beauty of its rivers, lakes and mountains. Outdoor activities include camping, fly and bait fishing, rock climbing, boating, hunting, and the winter sports of snowmobiling and cross country skiing.

While CA 49 does not cross Plumas County, CA70 crosses the county and is designated as the Feather River National Scenic Byway. The spectacular drive through the Feather River Gorge rivals any similar drive in North America.

Rich Bar, midway through the Feather River Gorge, was the richest river bar in California's Gold Rush Country. Plumas Eureka State Park, located just below the 7,490-foot Eureka Peak near Blairsden, is the highest of any in California's Gold Rush Country.

TOURING THE FEATHER RIVER NATIONAL SCENIC BYWAY

The Feather River Gorge begins about 10 miles north of Oroville in Butte County near Cherokee Road. From that point, the Feather River National Scenic Byway climbs steadily, passing former mining camps of Yankee Hill and Concow. Take time to observe the panorama of the Feather River Canyon to the south at the Grand View Vista Point.

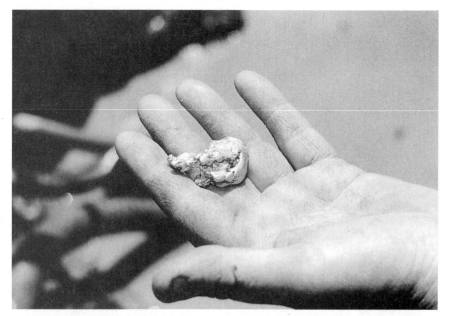

Gold nugget from Rich Bar.

Continue north for 4 miles of twisting and curving roads. Suddenly, the Feather River appears far below on the right side. Ahead, almost at eye level, is one of the major engineering feats of modern road building. The Pulga Bridge is 680 feet long and soars some 200 feet above the Feather River.

From this point, vistas appear at each turn in the road. The Feather River, far below, has been harnessed to provide electricity and no longer runs wild. During the winter and spring, however, the river does run at high levels with spectacular cascades over rocks in the riverbed.

At 2 miles north of Belden, the East Branch of the North Fork of the Feather River joins the North Fork. The Feather River National Scenic Byway (CA70) follows the East Branch to Quincy. At Rich Bar Road, 4 miles beyond Belden, turn right and descend the steep road down to Rich Bar.

RICH BAR

Rich Bar was discovered by members of the "Gold Lake" rush in July of 1850. Rich Bar proved to be the richest river bar in California's Gold Rush Country with more than 4 million dollars in gold taken out.

Miners could often find hundreds of ounces of gold in a single day at Rich Bar. While this small bar on the East Branch of the North Fork of the Feather River was rich in gold, one of its residents, Louise Amelia

Pulga Bridge crosses the Feather River.

FEATHER RIVER GORGE

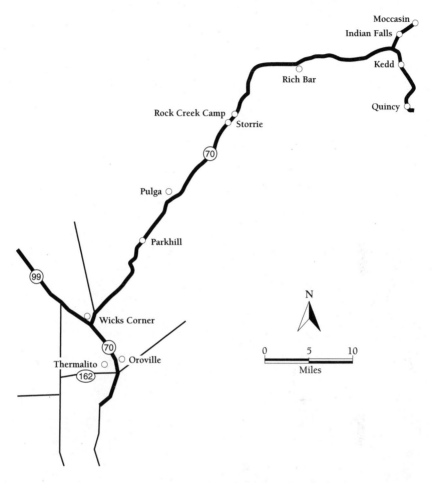

Knapp Smith Clappe (better known as Dame Shirley), provided scholars with a rich and detailed account of daily life in a river bar camp. From her arrival in September 1851 with her husband, Fayette Clappe, a Doctor, until her departure in late 1852, she wrote in exquisite detail about every facet of life—and death—at Rich Bar.

The tranquil scene found today at Rich Bar belies the crowded scene depicted by Dame Shirley: The small river bar boasted the Empire Hotel, the Indiana Boarding House, and a number of saloons and stores, in addition to the tents of the miners who crowded into the small area. Curtis Bancroft, with his young wife, Louise, moved to Rich Bar from Long Bar on the Yuba River to operate The Empire Hotel The hotel was a wood and canvas structure with 2 floors. Curtis's brother, Hubert Howe Bancroft, later recorded much of California's rich history in the late 1800s.

Digging at Rich Bar yields large nuggets.

RICH BAR

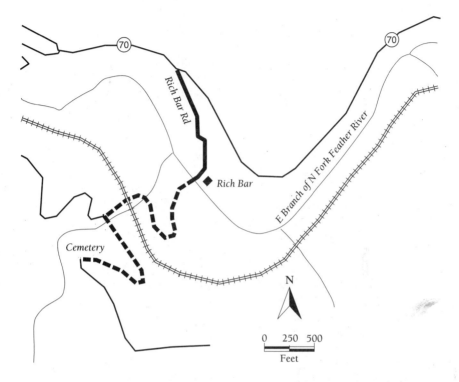

The 23 letters from "Dame Shirley" to her sister Molly in Massachusetts, written in 1851 and 1852, were published by *The Pioneer*, a San Francisco monthly magazine, in 1854 and 1855. Historians have been able to compare her lengthy manuscripts with diaries of others who visited Rich Bar during her time there to cross reference events. One of the best known diaries, which corroborates many of the incidents at Rich Bar, is that of Adolphus Windeler *The Gold Rush Diary of a German Soldier* edited by W. Turrentine Jackson. Indeed, Californian historians Josiah Royce and Hubert H. Bancroft acknowledged the importance of the Dame Shirley letters.

Bret Harte even used Dame Shirley's descriptions of incidents at Rich Bar as the basis for his "The Outcasts of Poker Flat" and "The Luck of Roaring Camp." Soon after Dame Shirley arrived at Rich Bar in 1851, Nancy Anne Bailey, 1 of the 2 other women in the camp died. Her grave marker stands in the small cemetery above the river bar where she died on September 30, 1851.

Rich Bar is now owned by Norman Grant. According to Grant, who operates the Rich Bar Mining Company, there is still much gold to be discovered in this small river bar. Visitors to Rich Bar can purchase buckets of dirt from Grant's own diggings or they can dig their own with hand tools. Almost every bucket yields flakes and even small nuggets, though this is not guaranteed. The Rich Bar Mining Company is open during warm weather months from early morning until sunset. During the winter, high water sometimes floods the bar and mining operations are usually closed.

Continue on the Feather River National Scenic Byway (CA 70) for twenty miles to Quincy. At the juncture of CA 89 with CA 70, the roadway leaves the Feather River and gradually moves into pine forests.

QUINCY

The scenic American Valley was first settled in 1852. One of the 3 founders of Plumas County selected his American Ranch as the site for Quincy, named after his hometown in Illinois. Spanish Peak, Spanish Creek, and Spanish Ranch were named for 2 Mexicans who settled there in 1850. The famed Monte Cristo Mine tunneled into Spanish Peak which reaches more than 7,000 feet at the west end of the American Valley. Livestock provide dairy products at several ranches in the valley.

Nestled in the center of the American Valley, Quincy is surrounded by forested mountains which provide a major source of income for the area. Virtually all of Plumas County is within the Plumas National Forest.

At Quincy, the Plumas County Museum has excellent displays of artifacts from Chinese miners, the Maidu Indians and pioneer life in the area. Plumas County Museum, 500 Jackson Street, P.O. Box 10766, Quincy, CA 95971; 916-283-6320. Hours: 8 A.M. to 5 P.M., Monday through Friday, year round and 10 A.M. to 4 P.M., on Saturday and Sunday, June to August. The first pioneer school house (1857) in Plumas County was moved to the Plumas County Fairground, 2 miles east of the Plumas County Courthouse in central Quincy.

Continue east on CA 70 for 2 miles to the Quincy–La Porte Road.

SIDE TRIP TO NELSON'S POINT, ONION VALLEY AND LA PORTE

Eight miles south of Quincy is Nelson's Point, at the confluence of Nelson Creek with the Middle Fork of the Feather River, where members of the Gold Lake rush found a rich strike of gold in 1850. La Porte is 30 miles farther by dirt road. For those with the time during the summer and the fall foliage season, this trip is an especially rewarding one with vistas at every turn of the road. The trip can easily be made in a car, provided that the road is dry.

A number of trails were opened to stagecoach roads through the region connecting Marysville with La Porte, and La Porte with Quincy and Johnsville. Each of these roads passes through scenic areas just as beautiful as when the 49ers traveled here. A number of the mountain peaks in

Plumas County Museum.

LA PORTE–ONION VALLEY SIDE TRIP

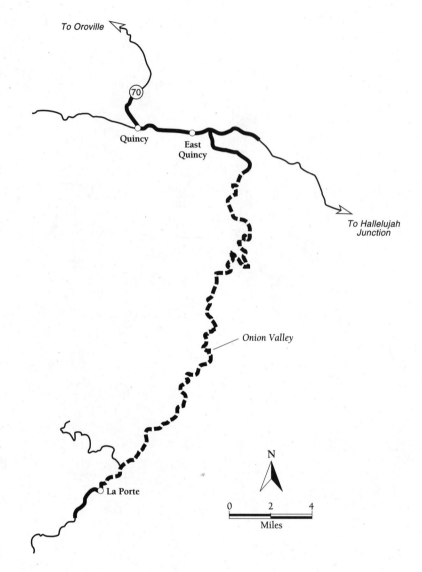

To Oroville

70

Quincy

East
Quincy

To Hallelujah
Junction

Onion Valley

La Porte

N

0   2   4
Miles

the area soar above the 7,000 foot mark. Onion Valley, on the La Porte–
Quincy Road near Pilot Peak, was found to be rich in gold deposits in
July 1850. The valley is named for the abundance of wild onions which
bloom after the snow melts in the summer.

In La Porte, the Union Hotel (1855) on Main Street is the dominant
building. It is not open to the public.

Before taking this side trip, be certain to obtain a good map of the area.
Return to CA 70 from La Porte.

Continue east for 20 miles on CA 70—much of the distance along the Middle Fork of the Plumas River—to Blairsden. Turn right and follow the signs for 3 miles to Plumas–Eureka State Park.

TOURING PLUMAS–EUREKA STATE PARK

The northernmost and highest in elevation, the Plumas–Eureka State Park is also the most scenic of the state parks in California's Gold Rush Country. In the shadow of 7,490-foot Eureka Peak, a number of mining operations commenced in 1851. By 1943, when the stamp mills fell silent, more than $25 million in gold had been removed from the 65 miles of tunnels in Eureka Peak.

Today, through an extensive preservation program that began in 1959, Plumas–Eureka State Historic Park is a shining gem in the California State Park System. The Plumas–Eureka Mill is undergoing long term renovation. An old bunkhouse serves as a museum building and numerous other buildings and equipment provide interpretive displays that allow a glimpse into Gold Rush activity at this mine.

The handmade snowshoes used by the legendary John "Snowshoe" Thompson, a native of Norway, are on display.

In adjacent Johnsville, a plaque notes that the area was the site of winter sports competitions beginning in 1860.

Stamp mill display at Plumas–Eureka State Park.

BECKWOURTH/SIERRAVILLE

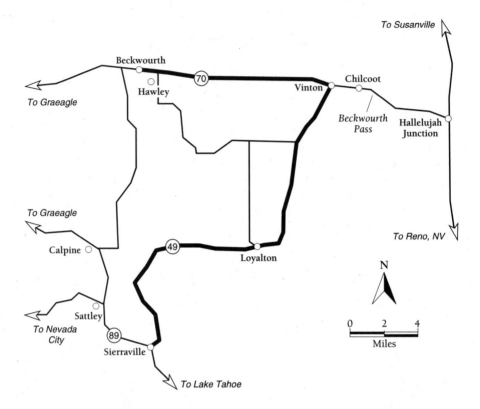

Visitors who plan to visit the Plumas–Eureka State Park in the winter should call ahead to determine if the road and the park are accessible. Plumas–Eureka State Park, 310 Johnsville Road, Blairsden, CA 96103; 916-836-2380; FAX 916-836-0498. Museum hours: 8 A.M. to 4 P.M., in summer; winter hours vary. Hours are subject to weather conditions, so call ahead.

Return to CA 70 and drive east for 15 miles to the western edge of the Sierra Valley.

BECKWOURTH PASS, BECKWOURTH TRAIL AND BECKWOURTH'S CABIN

James Beckwourth, also known as Beckwith, was a well known Black mountain man. An adventurer who joined a fur trapping expedition into the west in 1824, he became an accomplished explorer, trader, scout, and war chief of the Crow Indians. Eventually going west for the California Gold Rush, he participated in the Gold Lake rush in 1850.

BECKWOURTH CABIN

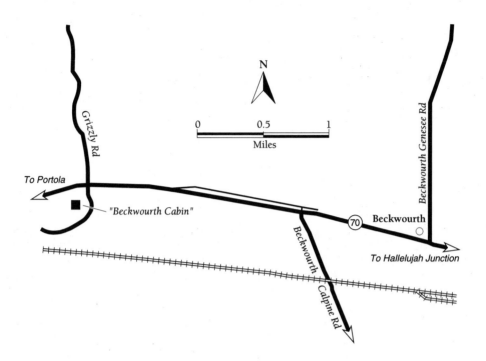

During this time, Beckwourth discovered what proved to be the lowest and easiest pass across the Sierra Nevada. Beckwourth Pass, at an altitude of only 5,221 feet, is located just east of Chilcoot, at the border of Plumas and Lassen County, at the eastern edge of the Sierra Valley. CA 70 crosses the Sierra Nevada at Beckwourth Pass. Unlike the better known passes farther south, the soil here is virtually rock free. Always an entrepreneur, Beckwith was able to persuade the City of Marysville to promise payment if he built a road from Beckwourth Pass, through the American Valley (now Quincy) to Marysville. He built the road but never received payment.

Beckwourth constructed a log cabin at the western edge of the Sierra Valley. Here he operated a trading post for emigrants using the Beckwourth Trail to reach Marysville.

Although some believe his cabin burned, a restored log cabin, believed to be that of Beckwourth, has been moved to Rocky Point Road, just off CA 70, 5 miles east of Portola. The cabin sits, without markings, 0.1 mile south of CA 70 on the west side of Rocky Point Road.

While the ownership of the cabin is uncertain, Beckwourth's contribution of the Beckwourth Pass Road far exceeded the remuneration for his efforts. Beckwourth left his cabin sometime during the 1860s and moved to Montana. He lived there with the Crow Indians until his death.

PLUMAS COUNTY TRAVEL INFORMATION

PLUMAS COUNTY VISITORS BUREAU
Telephone: 800-326-2247 or 916-283-6345; FAX 916-283-5465
Mailing Address: P.O. Box 4120, Quincy, CA 95971
Street Address: 91 Church Street

Chapter Eighteen

SHASTA COUNTY

From Redding, 165 miles north of Sacramento, drive west on CA 299, for 11 miles to Shasta State Historic Park.

SHASTA STATE HISTORIC PARK

First settled in 1849 as Readings' Springs, the town was renamed in 1850 as Shasta. During its glory days of the early 1850s, Shasta was a large gold-mining camp and also a major business and transportation hub for northern California. As an acknowledgment of its importance, Shasta was known as the "Queen City of the North."

The ruins of the Bull, Baker, and Company Building (1853) dominate the business area of Shasta on the south side of CA 299. 3 partners operated a supply business from this building that served much of northern California. One partner bought goods in San Francisco and shipped them up the Sacramento River to Red Bluff. A second partner transported the goods on wagons to Shasta City where the third partner sold them to the 49ers. While much of Shasta lies in ruins, well-marked remnants of the Gold Rush era provide a glimpse into its past.

On the north side of CA 299, 2 buildings remain from Shasta's glory days. The first is the 3-story Masonic Lodge (1854), originally built to house a mercantile business. The Masonic Lodge (Western Star Number Two) acquired the 3rd floor that same year and the entire building in 1859. The charter for Western Star Number Two was brought from Missouri by Peter Lassen (of Lassen Trail and Lassen County fame) in 1848.

SHASTA

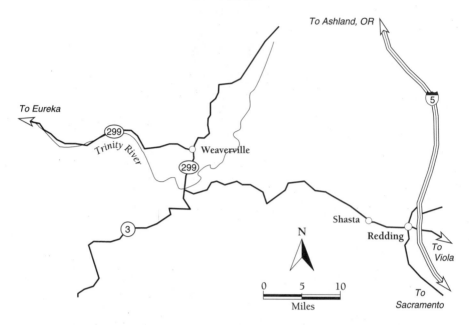

The second building is the renovated Shasta County Courthouse (1855). This building was the second county courthouse until Redding became the county seat in 1888. Today it serves as the Courthouse Museum and features Gold Rush memorabilia. Shasta State Historic Park, P.O. Box 2430, Shasta, CA 90687; 916-243-8194

Shasta State Historic Park is the beginning of the Trinity Scenic Byway designation for CA 299. The Byway stretches for 126 miles from here to Blue Lake near CA 101 at Arcata.

Continue west on CA 299 for 5 miles to the Whiskeytown Reservoir Visitor Center. Pause here to enjoy the beauty of the lake and its surrounding mountains. Deep beneath its waters lie the remains of the once thriving mining camp of Whiskeytown, founded in 1849.

Four miles west on the Trinity Scenic Byway (CA 299), turn right at Trinity Mountain Road (also called Main Street) to French Gulch. There are several Gold Rush era buildings here, including the French Gulch Hotel.

Continue west on the Trinity Scenic Byway (CA 299) to Trinity County.

SHASTA COUNTY TRAVEL INFORMATION

REDDING CONVENTION AND TOURIST BUREAU
Telephone: 800-874-7562; FAX 916-225-4354
Mailing and Street Address: 777 Auditorium Drive, Redding, CA 96001

Chapter Nineteen

TRINITY COUNTY

Trinity County is perhaps best known, outside of California's Gold Rush Country, for its scenic beauty. The Trinity Alps (north of Weaverville), the Trinity River (designated as the Wild and Scenic Trinity River) and numerous manmade and natural lakes make Trinity County an all season, outdoors sports paradise. The Trinity River yielded rich rewards to those 49ers who made the difficult trip to this area.

CA 299, which crosses Trinity County along much of the Trinity River Canyon, has been designated as the Trinity Scenic Byway in recognition of its scenic beauty. For some 35 miles, the Trinity Scenic Byway follows the course of the Wild and Scenic Trinity River. The scenic beauty of this area is rivaled by few other scenic areas in North America.

TOURING WEAVERVILLE

Weaverville, considered one of the most scenic locales in California's Gold Rush Country, is listed on the National Register of Historic Places. The nearby Trinity Alps form a picturesque background to Main Street's historic buildings. Weaverville was accessible only via pack trails until 1858 when a wagon road was built from Shasta. Weaverville appears much like it did during the Gold Rush.

The most unusual features that distinguish Weaverville from all other Gold Rush towns are the 3 circular iron staircases which lead to second floor balconies of a number of buildings. Each floor of these buildings had a separate owner which necessitated the building of outside staircases for access for those on the second floor.

WEAVERVILLE

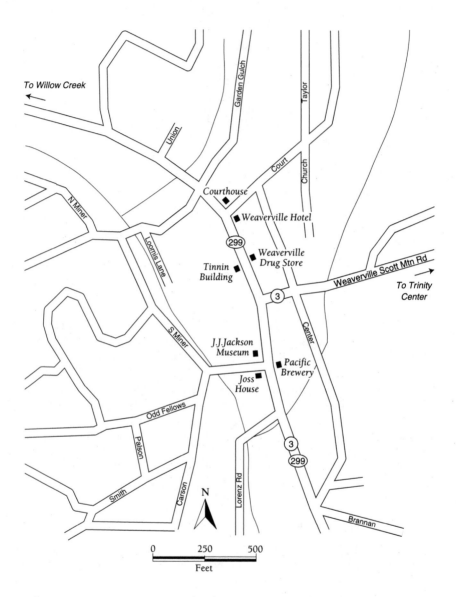

To Willow Creek

Garden Gulch

Taylor

Union

Court

Church

N Miner

Courthouse

Weaverville Hotel

Loomis Lane

299

Weaverville Drug Store

Tinnin Building

3

Weaverville Scott Mtn Rd

To Trinity Center

S Miner

J.J.Jackson Museum

Center

Pacific Brewery

Joss House

Odd Fellows

Palson

Carson

Smith

Lorenz Rd

N

3
299

Brannan

0   250   500
Feet

The Weaverville Drug Store, in business since 1852, is the oldest continuously operating drug store in California. The current building, built in 1855 to replace the original structure with a fireproof structure, still has the original woodwork and flooring. Take time to visit the drug store's "museum" which includes the wooden "shingle" (business sign) of H. B. Davison who founded the drugstore, and numerous other Gold Rush memorabilia.

Frank and Patricia Hicks, who operate the drug store and use the slogan of "Two Hicks Run the Weaverville Drug Store," will gladly provide you with a "mini-tour" of their artifacts. Patricia, historian and the author of several books about Weaverville, can answer just about any question you may have about the area. The Weaverville Drug Store, 219 Main Street, Weaverville, CA 96093; 916-623-4343.

The Trinity County Courthouse (1856) stands prominently at the north end of Main Street. The building first served as a hotel and saloon before being purchased by the county in 1865. The courthouse is distinguished as the second oldest courthouse in California's Gold Rush Country.

Morris & Company has been doing business in general merchandise since 1852 at 204 Main Street. The Trinity Journal, published weekly since January 26, 1856, occupies the Tinnin Building (1856) at 218 Main Street.

The Brewery Restaurant, in the Pacific Brewery Building (1855), is an excellent place for breakfast, lunch, or dinner in a historic setting, surrounded by an impressive collection of period antiques.

Some of the best beer in California's Gold Rush Country was produced in Trinity County after John and Christian Meckel settled in Helena, 15 miles west of Weaverville. Both came from the same area of Germany as Anhauser of the Anhauser-Busch Brewing Company. In fact, Anhauser and Christian Meckel are reported to have traveled together to California in 1852.

In 1878 when the Meckel Brothers dissolved their business relationship, John purchased the Pacific Brewery Building and continued brewing their Meckel Beer in Weaverville. According to the "Brewery Times," one Amos Gray, M.D., wrote in a United States Health Bulletin that:

> During the heated season people need a cooling bracing beverage. Such a palatable tonic must at once quench the thirst ... These U.S. Health Bulletins being the highest American authority on all matters pertaining to Health, Sanitation, and Hygiene, have just completed an unbiased and disinterested examination and analysis into many brands of beer, and the result of laboratory investigation has proven that the proper beer to drink and the purest and best to be the beer from Meckel Brothers Brewers of Weaverville, California.

Meckel Beer is no longer available, although other excellent California (and domestic and imported) beers can be purchased. The Brewery Restaurant, 401 South Main Street, Weaverville, CA 96093; 916-623-3000.

The Chinese Temple in Weaverville was built in 1874 to replace one built in 1852. Title was passed to the State of California in 1955 by one of the descendants of its builders, Moon Lim Lee, and is now preserved as the Weaverville Joss House State Historic Park. Its name, WON LIM MIAO ("Temple Amongst the Forest Beneath the Clouds"), is carved over its entrance. The museum houses numerous Chinese artifacts including some from the Tong War (1854) fought near here. Chinese from the Weaverville area as well as some of the 2,500 estimated to have worked in mining camps along the Trinity River worshipped before the ornate altar with the images of the gods of Health, Decision, and Mercy. Their descendants continue to worship here. Weaverville Joss House State Historic Park, 508 Main Street, P.O. Drawer 1217, Weaverville, CA 96093; 916-623-5284.

The J. J. Jackson Museum, at 402 Main Street, offers artifacts from pioneer families who settled the area. Hours: 10 A.M. to 5 P.M., daily, May through October. (916) 623-5211.

The Weaverville Hotel, 201 Main Street, has been in business since 1861. It operates in conjunction with Brady's Sport Shop. For room information, call (916) 623-3121.

The site of Oregon Gulch and the La Grange Mine, 4 miles west of Weaverville on the Trinity Scenic Byway (CA 299), is marked by a monitor on the south side of the road. In 1884, several existing mines were consolidated to form the La Grange Mine, one of the largest hydraulic mines in California's Gold Rush Country. At Junction City, there are huge piles of rocks, called tailings, stacked beside the Trinity River. They were put there as the result of extensive river dredging operations in the early twentieth century.

TOURING THE TRINITY RIVER MINING CAMPS

Numerous river mining camps were active along the Trinity River during the early 1850s. A favorite of fishermen, the fast flowing river is popular with white water rafting and kayaking enthusiasts. Lewiston, rich in gold at one time, is a popular fishing headquarters. A drive along the Trinity Scenic Byway (CA 299) from Junction City takes travelers through the scenic Trinity River Canyon. At Helena, there is an abandoned building that dates to 1859. Other one-time mining camps of Big Flat, Big Bar, French Flat, Del Loma and Cedar Flat have vanished into the river. At the confluence of the New River and the Wild and Scenic Trinity River, the road rises high above the canyon. The scenery is spectacular in this area.

SIDE TRIP TO GOLD BLUFFS BEACH

Reminiscent of the rush to the fabled "Gold Lake" in Sierra County, some 5,000 miners rushed to Gold Bluffs Beach on the Pacific Ocean in Humboldt County in the early 1850s after a miner reported golden nuggets the size of his fist scattered over the beach. Small nuggets were found but nothing near the size reported by the unidentified 49er. Today, eagles can be seen soaring overhead while elk graze along the edge of the sandy beach and on the sides of the golden bluffs.

For those who are traveling to the Redwoods or the Northern Coast of California, or who wish to make the complete odyssey through California's Gold Rush Country, Gold Bluffs Beach can be reached by traveling north on CA 101 to the small town of Orick (40 miles north of Eureka) in Humboldt County. Take the road to Prairie Creek Redwoods State Park to its end on the beach. Sunsets here are spectacular. Perhaps you may spot golden nuggets in the glow of the setting sun on Gold Bluffs Beach. Prairie Creek State Park, Orick, CA 95555; 707-488-2171.

TRINITY COUNTY TRAVEL INFORMATION

TRINITY COUNTY CHAMBER OF COMMERCE
Telephone: 800-421-7259 or 916-623-6101; FAX 916-623-3753
Mailing Address: P.O. Box 517, Weaverville, CA 96093
Street Address: 317 Main Street

Chapter Twenty

SAN FRANCISCO: TOWN BUILT BY GOLD

San Francisco is known as the town built by gold in recognition of its pivotal role during California's Gold Rush. San Francisco served as point of departure for 49ers who came by sea for the gold mines and for their return home. The young port was the major port of entrance for miners and mining supplies. The majority of the 49ers elected to return home by sea and departed from the Port of San Francisco. The San Francisco Mint processed much of the gold found in California for shipment by sea to the east coast.

San Francisco is, of course, an excellent place to begin or end your tour of California's Gold Rush Country.

A number of successful San Francisco businesses had their beginnings in the California Gold Rush. Notable among these are Levi Strauss & Co., Ghirardelli Chocolate Company, Wells, Fargo Bank, Bank of America, and Boudin Bread.

While in San Francisco, you can visit the Ghirardelli Chocolate Company Store at Ghirardelli Square. The Wells, Fargo Bank Museum, at 420 Montgomery Street, provides excellent displays of its history dating to the Gold Rush. Lotta Crabtree's Fountain was dedicated in 1875 by the famous dancer to the people of San Francisco. The fountain is located at Geary and Kearny Streets.

Boudin Bakery's sourdough bread, first served in San Francisco in 1849 by Isodore Boudin, is still baked fresh daily from flour, salt, water and the original mother dough that dates to the first loaf. Many consider

San Francisco sourdough to be the culinary byproduct of California's Gold Rush. Boudin Bakery outlets are located at Fisherman's Wharf, Ghirardelli Square, and elsewhere.

SAN FRANCISCO TRAVEL INFORMATION

THE SAN FRANCISCO TOURIST BUREAU
Telephone: 415-974-6900; FAX 415-227-2668
Street Address: 201 Third Street, Suite 900, San Francisco, CA

Chapter Twenty-One

SACRAMENTO: DREAMS OF NEW HELVETIA AND SUTTER'S FORT

Sacramento was founded at the confluence of the American and Sacramento rivers. It was near here that Sutter built a fort and made plans for a colony which he called New Helvetia. The site of Sutter's Fort, at 2701 "L" Street, is 1.5 miles east of downtown Sacramento. Now known as Sutter's Fort State Historic Park, the grounds and buildings of Sutter's Fort were restored between 1891 and 1893 by the State of California. The central building within Sutter's Fort is all that remains of the original structures.

Docents bring the history of Sutter's Fort and Sutter's dream of New Helvetia to life for its many visitors living demonstrations of daily life here. In addition to many artifacts from California's Gold Rush, displays at Sutter's Fort State Historic Park include tools used by James W. Marshall at Coloma and Kelsey, and memorabilia from the Donner Party. Sutter's Fort State Historic Park is open daily, from 10 A.M. to 5 P.M.. Fee; 916-324-0539

Old Sacramento, sandwiched between the banks of the Sacramento River and I-5, has a number of restored buildings in its several square block area. Several stern wheel paddle boats operate from the wharf along the riverfront. This area has extensive commercial shops and some museums. Notable are the California State Railroad Museum (111 "I" Street), the Discovery Museum (101 "I" Street), and the Wells, Fargo Museum (1000 Second Avenue).

The Crocker Art Museum at 216 "O" Street houses the art collection of Edwin B. Crocker of bank and railroad fame. The Crocker Art Mu-

Wells Fargo Museum.

seum Collection includes sketches and paintings by well known Gold Rush artists Charles Christian Nahl, Thomas Hill, and Albert Bierstadt. 916-264-5423.

Sacramento, in recognition of its economic and strategic importance, became the State Capital of California in 1854. The current Capitol, the third structure used by the State of California, was completed in 1874. The magnificent domed building dominates the downtown area of the fourth largest city in California.

SACRAMENTO TRAVEL INFORMATION

SACRAMENTO VISITORS BUREAU
Telephone: 916-264-7777; FAX 916-264-7788
Street Address: 1421 "K" Street, Sacramento, CA 95814

ABOUT THE AUTHOR

Since 1973, Les Kelly's photography and travel stories about the Amish, covered bridges, rural courthouses, and other Americana have appeared in numerous calendars, brochures, books, and more than eighty magazines in the United States of America, France, Germany, Italy, and Japan.

Kelly wrote and illustrated *California's Gold Rush Country* (Les Kelly Publications, 1997, ISBN 0-9653443-0-4) based on four years of extensive travel to and photography of all areas of California's Gold Rush Country. His research for that book provides the basis for *Traveling California's Gold Rush Country* He has published or provided photography for definitive photo books about Laura Ingalls Wilder, author of the *Little House* ® books including *Laura Ingalls Wilder Country* (HarperCollins 1990), *Musical Memories of Laura Ingalls Wilder* (Hear & Learn Publications 1992), *Little House Country: A Photo Guide to the Home Sites of Laura Ingall's Wilder* (Terrell 1989), *Laura Ingalls Wilder Country Cookbook* (HarperCollins September 1995), and *Little House Guidebook* (HarperCollins 1996). He co-authored *America's Amish Country* (America's Amish Country Publications 1992), a coffee table book depicting the Amish lifestyle in nineteen states and Ontario, Canada.

Kelly received his BA in English from McNeese State College (1966) and MBA in Management from McNeese State University (1970) . He lives in Huntington Beach, California, with his wife Catherine. He is a member of the Oregon–California Trail Association; Publicity Director, National Society for the Preservation of Covered Bridges; and, a former member of the Board of Directors, Laura Ingalls Wilder Home Association, Mansfield, Missouri.

Leslie A. Kelly at the 16-1 Mine, Alleghany.

FALCON has **FALCON** GUIDES® for hiking, mountain biking, rock climbing, walking, scenic driving, fishing, rockhounding, paddling, birding, wildlife viewing, and camping. Here are a few titles currently available, but this list grows every year. If you would like a free catalog with a complete list of available titles, call FALCON at the toll-free number at the bottom of this page.

SCENIC DRIVING GUIDES

Scenic Driving Alaska and the Yukon
Scenic Driving Arizona
Scenic Driving the Beartooth Highway
Scenic Driving California
Scenic Driving Colorado
Scenic Driving Florida
Scenic Driving Georgia
Scenic Driving Hawaii
Scenic Driving Idaho
Scenic Driving Michigan
Scenic Driving Minnesota
Scenic Driving Montana
Scenic Driving New England
Scenic Driving New Mexico
Scenic Driving North Carolina
Scenic Driving Oregon
Scenic Driving the Ozarks including the
    Ouchita Mountains
Scenic Driving Texas
Scenic Driving Utah
Scenic Driving Washington
Scenic Driving Wisconsin
Scenic Driving Wyoming
Back Country Byways
National Forest Scenic Byways
National Forest Scenic Byways II

Traveling California's Gold Rush Country
Traveler's Guide to the Lewis & Clark Trail
Traveling the Oregon Trail
Traveler's Guide to the Pony Express Trail

WILDLIFE VIEWING GUIDES

Alaska Wildlife Viewing Guide
Arizona Wildlife Viewing Guide
California Wildlife Viewing Guide
Colorado Wildlife Viewing Guide
Florida Wildlife Viewing Guide
Idaho Wildlife Viewing Guide
Indiana Wildlife Vewing Guide
Iowa Wildlife Viewing Guide
Kentucky Wildlife Viewing Guide
Massachusetts Wildlife Viewing Guide
Montana Wildlife Viewing Guide
Nebraska Wildlife Viewing Guide
Nevada Wildlife Viewing Guide
New Hampshire Wildlife Viewing Guide
New Jersey Wildlife Viewing Guide
New Mexico Wildlife Viewing Guide
New York Wildlife Viewing Guide
North Carolina Wildlife Viewing Guide
North Dakota Wildlife Viewing Guide

■ *To order any of these books, check with your local bookseller or call FALCON® at **1-800-582-2665***

Visit us on the world wide web site at:
http://www.falconguide.com

HIKING GUIDES

Hiking Alaska
Hiking Alberta
Hiking Arizona
Hiking Arizona's Cactus Country
Hiking the Beartooths
Hiking Big Bend National Park
Hiking Bob Marshall Country
Hiking California
Hiking California's Desert Parks
Hiking Carlsbad Caverns
    and Guadalupe National Parks
Hiking Colorado
Hiking the Columbia River Gorge
Hiking Florida
Hiking Georgia
Hiking Glacier & Waterton Lakes National Parks
Hiking Grand Canyon National Park
Hiking Great Basin
Hiking Hot Springs
    in the Pacific Northwest
Hiking Idaho
Hiking Maine
Hiking Michigan
Hiking Minnesota
Hiking Montana
Hiker's Guide to Nevada
Hiking New Hampshire
Hiking New Mexico
Hiking New York

Hiking North Cascades
Hiking North Carolina
Hiking Northern Arizona
Hiking Olympic National Park
Hiking Oregon
Hiking Oregon's Eagle Cap Wilderness
Hiking Oregon's Three Sisters Country
Hiking Pennsylvania
Hiking South Carolina
Hiking South Dakota's Black Hills Country
Hiking Southern New England
Hiking Tennessee
Hiking Texas
Hiking Utah
Hiking Utha's Summits
Hiking Vermont
Hiking Virginia
Hiking Washington
Hiking Wyoming
Hiking Wyoming's Wind River Range
Hiking Yellowstone National Park
Hiking Zion & Bryce Canyon National Parks
The Trail Guide to Bob Marshall Country
The Trail Guide to the Continental Divide
The Trail Guide to Glacier
The Trail Guide to Grand Canyon
The Trail Guide to Grand Teton
The Trail Guide to North Cascades
The Trail Guide to Olympic National Park

■ *To order any of these books, check with your local bookseller
or call FALCON® at* **1-800-582-2665**

Visit us on the world wide web site at:
http://www.falconguide.com

get FALCON GUIDED

BIRDING GUIDES
Birding Arizona
Birding Minnesota
Birder's Guide to Montana
Birding Texas
Birding Utah

FIELD GUIDES
Bitterroot: Montana State Flower
Canyonlands Wildflowers
Great Lakes Berry Book
New England Berry Book
Plants of Arizona
Rare Plants of Colorado
Rocky Mountain Berry Book
Tallgrass Prairie Wildflowers
Wildflowers of Southwestern Utah
Willow Bark and Rosehips

FISHING GUIDES
Fishing Alaska
Fishing Beartooths
Fishing Maine
Fishing Michigan
Fishing Montana
Fishing Yellowstone

HOW TO GUIDES
Bear Aware
Leave No Trace
Mountain Lion Alert
Wilderness First Aid

PADDLING GUIDES
Floater's Guide to Colorado
Floater's Guide to Missouri
Floater's Guide to Montana
Paddling Okefenokee Swamp
Paddling Oregon
Paddling Yellowstone

ROCK CLIMBING GUIDES
Rock Climbing Colorado
Rock Climbing Montana
Rock Climbing New Mexico & Texas

ROCKHOUNDING GUIDES
Rockhounding Arizona
Rockhound's Guide to California
Rockhound's Guide to Colorado
Rockhounding Montana
Rockhounding Nevada
Rockhound's Guide to New Mexico
Rockhounding Texas
Rockhounding Utah
Rockhounding Wyoming

MORE GUIDEBOOKS
Backcountry Horseman's Guide to
   Washington
Camping California's National Forests
Exploring Canyonlands &
   Arches National Parks
Recreation Guide to Washington
   National Forests

Trail Riding Western Montana
Wild Country Companion
Wild Montana
Wild Utah

WALKING
Walking Colorado Springs
Walking Portland
Walking St. Louis

■ *To order any of these books, check with your local bookseller*
*or call FALCON® at **1-800-582-2665***

FALCON®

Visit us on the world wide web site at:
http://www.falconguide.com

MOUNTAIN BIKING GUIDES

Mountain Biking Arizona
Mountain Biking Colorado
Mountain Biking New Mexico
Mountain Biking New York
Mountain Biking Northern New England
Mountain Biking Southern New England
Mountain Biking Utah

Local Cycling Series

Bozeman
Colorado Springs
Mountain Biking Bend
Mountain Biking Boise
Mountain Biking Chequamegon
Mountain Biking Denver/Boulder
Mountain Biking Durango
Mountain Biking Helena
Mountain Biking Moab

■ *To order any of these books, check with your local bookseller*
*or call FALCON® at **1-800-582-2665***

Visit us on the world wide web site at:
http://www.falconguide.com

WILDERNESS FIRST AID

By Dr. Gilbert Preston M.D.

Enjoy the outdoors and face the inherent risks with confidence. By reading this easy-to-follow first-aid text, all outdoor enthusiasts can pack a little extra peace of mind on their next adventure. *Wilderness First Aid* offers expert medical advice for dealing with outdoor emergencies beyond the reach of 911. It easily fits in most backcountry first-aid kits.

LEAVE NO TRACE

by Will Harmon

The concept of "leave no trace" seems simple, but it actually gets fairly complicated. This handy quick-reference guidebook includes all the newest information on this growing and all-important subject. This book is written to help the outdoor enthusiast make the hundreds of decisions necessary to protect the natural landscape and still have an enjoyable wilderness experience. Part of the proceeds from the sale of this book go to continue leave-no-trace education efforts. The Official Manual of American Hiking Society.

BEAR AWARE

by Bill Schneider

It's hardly news that Yellowstone is good habitat for both grizzly and black bears. Hiking in bear country can be very safe if hikers follow the guidelines summarized in this small, "packable" book. Extensively reviewed by bear experts, the book contains the latest information on the intriguing science of bear-human interactions. *Bear Aware* can not only make your hike safer, but it can help you avoid the fear of bears that can take the edge off your trip.

MOUNTAIN LION ALERT

By Steve Torres

Recent mountain lion attacks in California received national attention. Although infrequent, these and other lion attacks raise concern for public safety. *Mountain Lion Alert* contains helpful advice for mountain bikers, trail runners, horse riders, pet owners, and suburban landowners on how to reduce the chances of mountain lion-human conflicts.

To order these titles or to find out more about this new series
of books, call FALCON® at **1-800-582-2665.**